MW01142874

Future-Proofed: Your Guide to Acing High School, the College Application, and Beyond

Authored by John Andrew Williams
Illustrations by Lauren Waldinger

Published by
Institute of Academic Leadership
2000 North East 42nd Avenue, Suite 372
Portland, Oregon 97213

www.future-proofed.com

To Vick ~

Thank you for introducing Luois + me to the Enneagram. A big part of this book is owed to that personality system.

With love,
John

future-proofed

Dedicated to my Dad and Mom,
George and Patricia Williams,
for loving me with that crazy love
parents have for their kids

.

future-proofed

"The future belongs to those
who believe in the beauty of their dreams."

~ Eleanor Roosevelt

'fyoō-ch-er

proof'd:

Future-Proofed Defined

Future-proofed is not about knowing or controlling the future. That's impossible. It's not about getting a great SAT score or all A's. Being future-proofed requires skills that the SAT can't test and skills that can't be graded. It's not about making lots of money. Living a rich and fulfilling life goes far beyond having or not having lots of money. Being future-proofed is not about taking more classes and earning more academic degrees. Although a great foundation, degrees alone don't translate to being future-proofed.

Being future-proofed requires a mix of knowledge about how the world works as well as an awareness and knowledge about how you work. It asks you to be self-aware and treat others with deep respect. At times it demands you to be bold. At other times, humble. It challenges you to follow your passion while living a life in service to others.

Being future-proofed is having the skills, knowledge, and confidence to lead an effective, fulfilled adult life.

Schools traditionally have a hard time teaching these kinds of skills. It's not really the schools' fault. Their job is teaching core academic subjects, which are important and can be easily measured. For the most part they succeed. On the other hand, self-knowledge, leadership, communication, and motivation skills defy easy measurement yet are essential for students to learn to be future-proofed. This book focuses on these kinds of skills.

The skills in this book are more than just good ideas. Hundreds of students have successfully applied these concepts and skills in their lives. The results are proven.

Over the past five years, the average GPA gain for students who applied these skills and graduated from the Academic Life Coaching Program was 0.81 points *per semester* (for those students not already earning above a 3.5). Nearly every graduate of the program has been accepted to one or more of their top three college choices. I constantly get emails from program graduates thanking me for the skills they learned and the difference it has made in their lives.

The path to being future-proofed is clear. You're holding the road map in your hands.

Who this Book is For

This book is for students who want a roadmap to build the foundation and develop the skills necessary to be future-proofed.

It's for straight-A students who want to learn a more versatile set of skills.

It's for struggling students who want to find an easier way to get organized and take advantage of the opportunities that life provides.

It's for students who are stressed out by the college application and who want to learn a better way to approach it.   It's for parents who want to future-proof their children and teach them a different kind of skill set not emphasized in school.

It's for educators to use in a semester class, the beginning of an academic seminar, or class retreat.

It's for anyone who wants to be future-proofed or future-proof those they love.

Introduction

the gap

There is a gap between what's taught in schools and what's useful in life.

I fell into this gap when I graduated college and went directly into teaching. I started my professional career teaching high school Latin. With a newly minted college degree, I thought I was future-proofed. I thought school prepared me to meet the challenges and take advantage of the opportunities the world offered. It didn't. I simply wasn't prepared. Even worse, I realized the same thing was happening to the next generation of students. Students were going through the high school system not learning skills needed to live effective, fulfilled adult lives.

Determined to find a solution, I set out to discover the concepts, knowledge, and skills students needed to learn to be better prepared for the future.

After eight years of researching, testing, and refining, I gathered the essential concepts students needed to learn and developed a program that they could both understand and use in their lives. To date, I've worked with over 2,800 students and their families. I've spoken to hundreds of audiences. I've built a consulting company based in Portland, Oregon that includes consultants located as far away as Dubai, United Arab Emirates. And I write a weekly column in the education section of *Newsweek*.

I know what works in schools and in the real world. I know how to future-proof students, and I wrote this book to share that expertise with you.

the college application

Just mention the words "college application" and watch stress levels rise. It's unfortunate that the college application has turned into such an anxiety-filled rite-of-passage. It doesn't have to be that way.

You can take a deep breath. This book will help you get into a great school and thrive.

By design I did not include the whole list of recommended steps in the college application process or detailed tips on writing your best essay. To get that information, you can visit www.future-proofed.com and download free PDF's on essays, scholarships, college visits, and all the other tips and guidelines you could ever want.

The purpose of this book is to go a level deeper. It encourages you to learn the core skills necessary to give you the resilience to be future-proofed. It also provides a blueprint for you to build a stronger foundation and have a better high school experience. If you master these kinds of skills, getting outstanding grades and getting into the college you want is the easy part. I've seen it. Students who apply these skills consistently beat the long odds of getting accepted to selective schools. Students who would have given themselves a slim chance of even going to college not only get accepted but thrive.

future-proofed

From my perspective, these skills come before the tips and tools of the college application process. Learn the core concepts, master the basics, and all the other pieces will fall into place.

how to use this book

You can use this book individually or in a group. You may find that reading this book in a group offers a richer experience and allows you to benefit from the support of others.

The book is designed to be used in a semester class and for each of the chapters to prompt you to move into action. Whether you go through the book individually or with a group, it's a good idea to have others hold you accountable to moving forward.

You can skip around or read straight through it, but the chapters do build on themselves. As you find yourself getting more comfortable with the material, you'll find that the book, much like life, is more cyclical than linear. After you finish reading the book, you'll find it useful to go through each of the exercises in the chapters again with the knowledge of what comes later. The real work is in applying the concepts in your life, not just understanding them.

Now let's get to it.

You

Skill #1: Your ability to be self-aware and fully authentic.

take the pressure off

The first step to being future-proofed is to take the pressure off. You don't need to be something or someone you think you need or should be. Doing so is a recipe for stress and disappointment. The most valuable thing you can do is to be totally and completely you. Yet, so many students are stressed out and have their identities tied up with their academic performance and where they get into college. It's understandable. The average high school student has nearly fifteen homework assignments, three quizzes, and two tests a week. That's about 720 assessments a school year and 2,800 in four years of high school. In addition, students have a report card mailed home to their parents every nine weeks and have to undergo the coming-of-age-SAT/ACT initiation. Good luck with not associating your identity with how well you do. By the way, what's your SAT score?

Just kidding. Relax. Take a deep breath. Everything is, and will be, OK. Getting good grades and SAT scores and getting into a great college is important. This book will show you a different, better way than the pressure cooker most high school students find themselves in.

Allowing yourself to simply be yourself with all your personality quirks and interests and bad jokes and whatever it is that makes you "you" is one of the most important skills you can develop to make yourself future-proof.

Many people spend the first decade of their life after they graduate college trying to refigure out who they are and what they want to do with their lives. Psychologists have even coined the term "quarter life crisis" for the phenomenon of 25-year olds freaking out because they don't know much about who they are or how they fit into society.

The natural response to figuring out your future is to try harder, to struggle, to be more ambitious, and to meet high expectations set by yourself and others. That's one way. But it produces a ton of stress and leads many to the quarter-life crisis.

There's a better way. It helps to remember that you are enough. You are unique. You have a place in this world, and a very important place at that. Your job is not to compare yourself to others or to constantly outdo your classmates.

Your job is to be so fully you that you shine. It's to go after what you love to do, to fully apply yourself, and enjoy your talents. Doing so is the foundation of being future-proofed.

get real

"If I had to give any advice on writing a college application essay, it's be real. Don't try to be tricky or impressive. Authenticity goes a long way to being likable, and being likable is exactly what we were looking for."
- Justin Carroll, a former admissions officer at Brown University

Just like fake cheese, fake people don't win a lot of fans. We like people who are real. When people are too polished or when an essay makes someone seem too perfect, it comes across as hollow and mechanical.

We like people who are authentic with all their flaws and imperfections and fears and silly hopes just like we have. It makes us human. It makes us likable. It makes life interesting and fun. It also makes for a great college application essay.

Being real is an act of courage. It means naming the elephant in the room. It requires you to face your shortcomings and be honest about your weaknesses. It also means being honest with yourself about your talents and gifts. It means talking about something that's really important to you and engaging in conversations that go

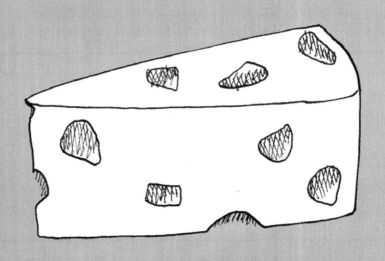

beyond how things are going.

With thousands of subtle and not-so-subtle messages about who you should be sent daily across computer, movie, and television screens, knowing who you are and what's really important to you is not just useful, it's essential to being future-proofed.

personality tools

The number of personality tools and typing tests is endless. Some of them have more merit than others.

At their best, typing systems give you insight into your personality, raise your awareness about useful and not-so-useful patterns, and help you communicate better.

At their worst, they make you feel pigeonholed, bad about yourself, or mad that you wasted your time. Like any tool, if it's not working, stop and put it down.

Just like the map is not the territory and some maps are better than others, personality typing systems are not your personality, and some systems are better than others. The key with personality tests is to have fun. Explore different typing systems. Don't take them too seriously, but take them seriously enough to gain value from them.

One of my favorites is Number Typing. To find your Number Typing visit www.future-proofed.com and download the six page PDF *Choosing Your Type*. Finding your personality type is easy. You simply read each of the nine paragraphs and pick out which one best describes you. (By the way, I'm a Number Type 7. What number are you?)

You'll find there's a certain peace that comes with a better understand and more knowledge about yourself. It's a great feeling and essential to being future-proofed.

thinking styles

Ever wonder why some teachers seem to be really good for some students and terrible for others? Usually it's caused by a simple match or mismatch of academic thinking styles. Just like students, each teacher has a bias for their own style. If your styles line up, you're in luck. If they don't, it could create problems.

The brain is built for gathering information, solving problems, and making decisions. Because brains like to store information efficiently, it stores information in categories it can easily understand. Like a good reporter, the brain codes information into these categories:

- Who?
- What?
- When?
- Where?
- Why?
- How?

Academically, the big three questions brains like to know are:

- What?
- Why?
- How?

We can, of course, think and be comfortable with all three academic thinking styles. But usually one of the three makes us feel most comfortable and we have a preference for that kind of thinking. It's easy to find your own style. Look back at a paper you recently wrote or think about which question you most want to know the answer to when you're at a presentation.

What-people want to know is more details and information. They believe that if they know more about the subject then they can easily understand why or how something happened.

Why-people want to know the reasons behind the action. They take the details or how something happened for granted. They trust that if they know why something works, they can figure out many ways how to do it and all the details will be obvious.

How-people usually don't care much about the details or why something works. They really want to know how it happened and how they can do it for themselves. They think if they can understand how to do it, the details and the reasons why it works will become clear.

Most students and teachers don't know their bias in thinking styles. It's unfortunate. But now that you know about thinking styles and know your own style, you can take steps to make studying and getting great grades easier.

applying thinking styles

The key to applying thinking styles is to get comfortable with each style and learn to recognize the kind of organization each style creates. The next step is to make sure you cycle through each style when taking notes, studying, and writing.

Take Chris for example. He was entering the Spring semester of his Junior year when I started working with him. He was gearing up for AP Tests, but he was frustrated by the practice exams. On the practice tests, he would get a 5 on the multiple-choice sections, but when it came to the essays he couldn't get above a 3. His AP US History teacher thought Chris's writing was strong on details but needed more analysis and explanation.

Chris was a clear what-person. He thought he knew a subject when he knew many details about it, and his essays became an exercise in facts and details. He didn't spend much time addressing the reasons why or how events happened. To a why- or how-person, Chris's essays lacked depth and analysis.

Once Chris learned to take into account and include the *why* and the *how* in his essays, he took his writing to the next level, earning 5's on his APs and a 760 on his SAT writing section.

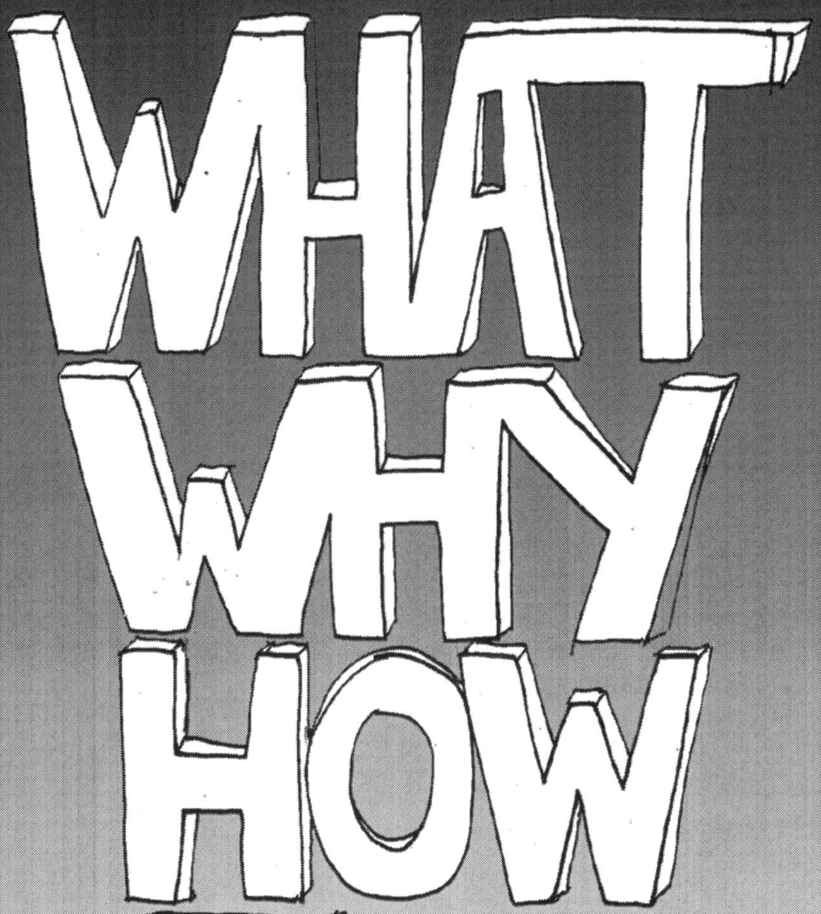
WHAT
WHY
HOW
THINK!

To give you an example of what cycling through each academic style looks like, here's an excerpt from the Wikipedia article on the American Revolution:

(1)The revolutionary era began in 1763, when the French military threat to (2) British North American colonies ended.

(3) Adopting the policy that the colonies should pay an increased proportion of the costs associated with keeping them in the Empire, Britain imposed a series of direct taxes followed by other laws intended to demonstrate British authority, all of which proved extremely unpopular in America. (4) Because the colonies lacked elected representation in the governing British Parliament, many colonists considered the laws to be illegitimate and a violation of their rights as Englishmen. (5) In 1772, groups of colonists began to create committees of correspondence, which would lead to their own Provincial Congresses in most of the colonies. In the course of two years, the Provincial Congresses or their equivalents rejected the Parliament and effectively replaced the British ruling apparatus in the former colonies, (6) culminating in 1774 with the coordinating First Continental Congress.[1]

---

1 http://en.wikipedia.org/wiki/American_Revolution

This paragraph is a perfect example of each primary academic thinking style, including the extra bonus of *when* and *where*. Read through again and notice at each number, the author shifts through each of the thinking styles.

     (1) *When*
     (2) *Where*
     (3) *What*
     (4) *Why*
     (5) *How*
     (6) *What*

It's almost poetry. Using the academic thinking styles not only leads to stronger writing, it ensures you reach your audience, no matter their thinking style.

The same level of care to thinking style applies to your college application, SAT, AP, and other essays. It also works with Math, Science, and Foreign Languages. Once you're aware of your style and begin to develop the others, you'll notice that you not only get better at school, school becomes a lot easier too.

learning styles

Learning styles function very much like academic thinking styles. The brain likes to code information in ways it can efficiently use, and knowing your learning style makes it possible for you to work with, rather than against your brain.

There's a lot of information on learning styles. To download a complete learning styles assessment and tool kit visit www.future-proofed.com. In the meantime, the following simple explanations of the big three learning styles - audio, visual, and kinesthetic - have been the most useful for students to know.

1) **Visual:** Visual learners learn best by seeing the concepts drawn out, either on paper or in their heads. When reading they may or may not sub-vocalize (hear a little voice in their head sound out the words softly). They like speakers and teachers to stand still when leading class. Visual learners are usually good spellers and learning visually is the most efficient of the learning styles.

2) **Audio:** Audio learners take in information best by hearing it. When reading they always sub-vocalize and tend to be slower readers than visual learners. They also learned how to spell by sounding out the words. Audio

learners tend to be strong in working in groups and generating ideas verbally.

3) **Kinesthetic:** Kinesthetic learners learn best by doing or experiencing what they are learning. When reading they find their imaginations want to act out the action. They also tend to be slow readers, and learn to spell by writing out the words over and over. Kinesthetic learners communicate well with body-language and feel most comfortable working with their hands and on projects.

It's important to remember, we each use all three learning styles but one or two of them are dominant. Once you know your learning style you can use it to your advantage.

Traditional school favors visual learners. It's tough news if learning visually is not your strength, but the good news is that you can also develop and improve other learning styles. Think of it like taking your brain to the gym. (You can find exercises on www.future-proof.com.)

Once you get in the habit of using various learning styles at different times, you'll find it easier to learn from a variety of teachers, which is always a good thing.

you and the college application: aim for likability on your college essay

Stop trying to get into the most prestigious university you can. It usually only frustrates you and leads to college applications that seem phony or overly-impressive-ish. Avoid the temptation.

Think instead of finding the college that best fits you. It takes off a lot of pressure. It makes you curious about all the departments, details, and feel of each university. Your focus naturally shifts from trying to fit into a box to finding the box that best fits you.

You'll also be giving admission officers what they are really after, a genuine look at who you are as a person. They want to like you. They want to fall in love with your application and admit you. All you have to do is be totally, 100% you, and you'll be genuine. People like genuine. Genuine is enough. I've seen hundreds of application essays, and I know that the ones I like are the most genuine and honest. It's not surprising that those kinds of essays also earn the best acceptance rates.

A common question comes up, "What do I write about in my college essay?" and "How do I get started?"

First visit the Common Application site and find the available essay topics.[2] Think about them for a moment and ask yourself a simple question, "Which one would I have the most fun writing?"

After you've picked your topic here are a few guidelines:

- Give yourself an hour to free write. Write anything that comes to mind. Any funny story. Anything at all. Then put it aside for a day and come back to it. There's usually some gems in there and it's a great way to start.
- Pick one time or story in your life and write a narrative about it.
- Include actual quotations if you can remember them.
- Involve the senses with details.
- If you can pull it off, humor is great.
- Minimum, one page. Maximum, two pages. (Seriously, not one word more than two pages.)
- Avoid clichés.
- Write your essay the summer before your senior year.

---

2 http://www.commonapp.org. About 415 colleges are member colleges and accept the Common Application. Many other colleges are not, but the prompts found in the Common App are similar to what many other colleges ask on their own applications.

- Have fun with it. After you write it, if you have the urge to re-read it over and over, you know you have a great essay.

The bottom-line is that when you are real, tell a great story and tell it well, you give admission officers the best chance they have to get to know and like you. When they like you, that's your best chance for getting an acceptance letter.

Vision

Skill #2: Your ability to create a clear, positive vision of the future.

E

ZNQT

VISION

HFGZTSQC

XGFTHNLAY2W

the concrete benefits of a vision story

The best way to future-proof yourself for the future is to take a proactive stance in creating it. Learning how to create and use effective vision statements is the first step to becoming future-proof. When you use your imagination to put yourself into your ideal reality, you create direction in your life. It keeps you focused when faced with distractions. It helps you make better decisions. It gives you direction and a mission, making you a more compelling leader. It helps you keep moving even when things are tough, one of the most important indicators that you are future-proof.

Olympic athletes know the benefit of creating a vision story to give them an edge over the competition. Shaun White, a two-time gold medalist, visualizes his runs before dropping in the half-pipe.[3] Many athletes imagine themselves standing on the podium with their national anthem playing. Several studies have been published and replicated that show measurable increases in performance when athletes use concrete vision stories.[4]

So how does this apply to a high schooler? Let's consider a real-life example of Emily, an 11th grader who

---

[3] http://www.podiumsportsjournal.com/2010/02/15/sport-psychology-at-the-winter-olympic-games-vancouver-2010/

[4] http://www.podiumsportsjournal.com/2007/12/21/pettlep-imagery---a-new-frontier-in-mental-conditioning/

was having a hard time picking classes for her senior year and staying interested in school. She wanted to graduate with good grades, get into a good college, and become a doctor. But she simply wasn't excited about the rest of high school.

Emily took creating a vision story seriously. She imagined herself looking at her report card and feeling the satisfaction of earning great grades. She visualized herself after she graduated medical school and when she started working with patients. She added detail: what it would be like to hold her diploma, the look on her patients' faces after she helped them get better, the thank-you's she received, and the look and feel of her office.

Suddenly what was a far-off reality, having her own practice and having a positive impact on the lives of others, became real, almost tangible. As we continued to work together through her senior year and college application process, we often referred to her vision when she needed to remember why she was putting in hard work.

The results were impressive. After she received her acceptance letters from multiple colleges, Emily's mother jokingly said to me, "I wish she would at least get a rejection letter or two to bring her down to reality."

The truth is that creating a vision story like Emily's has a big impact on reality.

how to create a vision story

The biggest challenge to creating a vision statement is knowing what you're aiming for (and what you're not). An effective vision statement is similar to a goal, but it has a subtle and important difference. A goal is usually a short statement of what you want to achieve. A vision statement is how good it will be once you achieve it and reminds you why you are putting in the effort. It is not a daunting, over-arching, meaning-of-life statement that has to perfectly reflect your entire life's purpose. A vision statement is much simpler, more useful, and a lot less stressful.

There's no right or wrong way to create a vision statement, but there are guidelines. An effective vision statement has four characteristics. It's written down, focused on a specific experience, fun to reread, and inspires by engaging your senses. You can also play with recording your vision statement and listening to it.

Write it down

I know, writing things down doesn't always generate a lot of enthusiasm, but a certain magic happens when you commit something to paper and can refer to it later. It's a little bit of effort that makes a big difference. Plus, it's great fun to go back and read vision statements that you wrote years ago seeing how they match up to what actually happened.

Keep it focused

Focus on the actual event and the experience you'll have. With one event in mind you free yourself from the pressure-laden task of capturing your entire life's purpose in one statement. It also makes it easy to fill out details and make it real. What will it really be like to have achieved that project early? How good would it be to see your report card filled with A's? How good would it feel in the morning to know for sure that you've got all your homework finished and you're 100% prepared for the day? It'd feel pretty awesome. Now write all that goodness down.

A few focused, descriptive sentences go a long way.

Make it Fun

A vision statement is only as good as you use it, and we use things that are fun. After you write it, do you want to read it again and again? Does it bring a smile to your face? Is it something that you'll want to pick up many times throughout the day? If not, dig a little deeper and find that thing that really makes it pop for you. The key is likely to be found in what would be fun, exciting, and breaking new ground for you.

Inspire by Engaging the Senses

A vision statement is only good if it moves you to action. Does it include imagery like what you will see, hear, or touch? Does it warm your heart and mention the emotion you'll feel once you've met your accomplishment? Does it inspire you? You know you have a good vision statement if reading or hearing it makes you want to jump out of your seat and get to work achieving your vision.

After you've created your vision story and commit to reading or listening to it, get ready to have surreal, pinch-me-am-I-dreaming moments. I've seen it and experienced it dozens of times. When you actually experience a story that you've only dreamed about, you'll realize how powerful this skill is. That experience is your future-proofed future.

delayed gratification

Delaying gratification doesn't sound like a barrel of fun. It's not. But if you have a solid vision story, it makes it that much easier to put in the work now for benefit later. Learn to do that, and you're well on your way to being future-proofed.

In an experiment conducted in the late 1960's and followed-up in the 1980's, Professor Walter Mischel, a researcher at Stanford University, demonstrated how important the ability to delay gratification was to long-term success. His study was simple. A researcher presented a four-year old with a simple decision, "You can have one marshmallow now or you can wait until I return and have two marshmallows." [5]

A hidden camera caught the action while the researcher stepped out of the room. Imagine the agony of a four-year-old all alone in the room with the marshmallow in hand, tempted to eat the marshmallow but knowing that if she held out, she'd get two! (There's great YouTube footage.) Professor Mischel found about a third of the children gave in under 30 seconds after the researcher left

5 Mischel, W., & Ayduk, O. (2004). "Willpower in a cognitive-affective processing system: The dynamics of delay of gratification". In R. F. Baumeister & K. D. Vohs (Eds.), Handbook of self-regulation: Research, Theory, and Applications (pp. 99-129). New York: Guilford.

the room. Another third held out a few long minutes. The last third were able to hold out for the entire 15.

The real brilliance of the study was to follow-up 12 years later when the four-year olds were then in high school. The differences in the performance between those who waited the full 15 minutes versus those who didn't hold out for even 30 seconds was distinct. Those who were able to delay gratification and earn two marshmallows had fewer behavioral problems, were more satisfied in their friendships, and earned on average 210 points higher on their SAT scores.

The benefits of learning to delay gratification are real, and the first step is to create a clear vision of how awesome the future is going to be if you put in the work now.

Greg Bell, author of *Water the Bamboo*, describes the experience of farming a certain kind of timber bamboo. After the farmer plants a seed, he must spend the next two years watering the seed diligently without seeing any sign of growth. Two years is a long time to continue to put in work without seeing any sign that it's working. But then once the bamboo starts to grow, it grows an astonishing 90 feet every 60 days. It grows so fast you can actually hear the plant adding height. You can imagine the incredible effort and faith the farmer must have. You can also imagine the incredible profit the farmer then enjoys.

The same awesome results of putting in work now for reward later applies to your life. The scales tip and a project starts to flow, as a result of months, even years of effort. Having a strong vision story reminds you why it is worth it to delay gratification. Like the four year-olds imagining the joy of two marshmallows or the farmer diligently watering for his future bamboo, you too must become willing to endure long-term work for longer-term gain. Having a vision story and a willingness to work towards it are the first signs that you're becoming future-proofed.

WHATS BEHIND DOOR # 1 ?

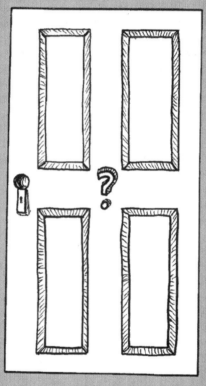

leadership: a vision for yourself and others

At the foundation of effective leadership is the ability to create a positive vision for yourself and others. As you become more comfortable creating vision stories for yourself, the next step is to dream a little bigger and imagine the positive impact you can have on the lives of others.

Too many people focus on the actual "leadership position" as evidence of their being a leader. Worse, students try to gain "leadership experience" to look good on college applications. It used to work, but then everyone started listing their leadership positions. It no longer distinguishes you from the herd. What does call attention to your leadership potential is undertaking a project or gathering a group of people together that fills a real need outside of what schools typically offer. The best reason to step into leadership is because you want to serve others better. Such a desire starts by seeing the need in your own life and in the lives of others. The next step is to take action to fill the need.

Find that need. Create a vision of how good it could be. Take steps to fill the need. You'll soon find that you're on your way to becoming an outstanding leader. College admission officers can tell the difference between someone who is going through the motions to get the recognition and someone who is fueled by passion.

Effective leadership comes from identifying a need and serving others as you would yourself. There is no higher calling. It's the reason why leadership is such a highly regarded concept.

Look for the need

To apply this in your life, start to look for the need. You realize your school is missing a club, so you create one. You realize your family could use a vacation so you plan it. You realize you (or a friend) need to do better in math, so you find a tutor.

I've seen high school students plan complete educational sections for elementary school students, put on plays and performances to raise money for local and national charities, as well as start clubs that really meet the needs of students and gain 20 members in a week. Once you find a need and create a vision of how it could be different, get ready to communicate that vision to others and move into action. You're taking the first steps in exercising effective leadership.

Here are some questions to get you started:

future-proofed

In your life, what's needed?

In your family, what's needed?

In your group of friends, what's needed?

In your community, what's needed?

the game designs the player

Once you determine the need you want to fill, don't be intimidated by how large or ambitious your project may be. Just take the next step and trust that you'll know what to do.

Human beings are designed to adapt to challenges. Choose to fill a challenging need and your project will dictate what you need to learn, how you need to grow, what resources you need to gather, and what skills you need to develop.

From a traditional academic perspective, the school's job is to give you all the skills you need before you have a need to apply them. In other words, the learning comes before the need. Outside of school, most people learn what they need to when faced with a challenge. In other words, the need comes and then you learn.

You can trust that life will teach you what you need to learn. Your job is to allow the game to design you. Don't fight the game.

Being future-proof requires that kind of mental flexibility. It's not just that you're OK with being flexible and learning new skills as the need arises, it's that you *expect* it.

You get to pick your game, but the game designs you. The quality of who you become is equal to the quality of the game you decide to play.

be in it for the long-haul

Be in it for the long-haul. Your long-range view gives you the benefit of avoiding the optimist/pessimist game.

When things are tough and don't go your way, it's tempting to think that things will always be dire and hopeless. Especially when you're tired, stressed out, and over-committed, bad news has a larger impact.

Same goes for positive news. When things are going your way, it's also tempting to think that once that one big thing comes through, all your problems are gone forever. Unfortunately, it's not true.

The reality is that things will not be forever rainy or sunny, but you'll forever get a mixture of both. By being in it for the long-haul, you avoid the trap of allowing the most recent events from coloring the way you see the reality of the situation.

Taking steps forward involve some measure of mistakes, failure, ease, and success. Mistakes are inevitable. Things won't always go the way you want. In the same way, success is inevitable too. Things are bound to go your way if you keep moving forward.

The key is to keep moving forward, no matter the external circumstances. If you're in it for the long-haul and have a strong vision story, you'll be in a better position to address what needs to be addressed and do what needs be done.

applying vision stories to the college application process

Getting in the habit of creating strong vision stories takes your high school experience and the college application to the next level. It has two main benefits. First, it naturally helps you become a better candidate. Second, it helps you keep motivated to complete all the pieces of your application before you're up against deadlines, which tend to sap quality.

I help students get into the best colleges for them, and I've had a lot of success doing it. One of the most powerful exercises I've seen students use is the creation of a vision story. Students who've used this tool have turned around their grades, performed better on the athletic field, and earned admission to elite schools.

If you apply this tool, you'll soon find yourself naturally doing your homework on time, being a leader, and creating projects that fill a need. The challenge is to apply it consistently while keeping faith in your vision and continuing to take action.

Colleges are really looking for those kinds of authentic leadership roles, not the list of activities and leadership positions that many students think count. Who really cares if you were the president of such-and-such a club or captain of the varsity team? So were 50,000 other students. College admission officers care if you actually stepped up and did something outside the normal path of a high school student that had a real impact on your own life and the lives of others.

Another benefit of getting in the habit of creating vision stories is that you're more likely to be curious and start thinking about the future in a productive way. You begin to think, "What would that actually be like?" instead of having a vague notion of what it's like to be a marine biologist. No one, especially college admission officers, expects you as a high school student to have a crystal clear idea of what you want to do for the rest of your life.

It's helpful, however, if you've at least thought about it and taken some real steps to see if what you're interested in is really for you. Call up a lawyer, doctor, professional musician, marine biologist, or forensic scientist and ask them what it's really like. You'll gain insight into their profession and find out if it's a good fit for you. Colleges are more interested in students who show that kind of resourcefulness and thoughtfulness about their future.

On a practical level of filling out an application, it can be challenging to keep motivated to get things done well before due dates (which is VERY helpful) without a clear vision story of where you're going and why you're doing all this work. So many students get caught up in comparing themselves to others, procrastinating on writing their essays, and asking for recommendations only at the last minute. Really getting into your vision story of what you want your experience to be like avoids much of the stress and many of the problems usually associated with the college application. It puts you on a path that's your own.

Perspectives

Skill #3: The ability to identify, create, and choose both negative and positive perspectives.

perspectives matter

Imagine it's the first day of the second semester. You're about to meet your new teacher. As you walk into the classroom, a few students are filling out evaluations from their last class with the same teacher. Their evaluations overflow with positive comments. They all speak highly of the teacher as they exit. Do you think their positive perspective would make a difference in how you approach the class?

What if the opposite happened? Imagine that instead of a glowing report, the students evaluating the teacher wrote that the teacher was horrible, hard to understand, and not effective. Do you think it would make a difference in your performance?

Feldman and Prohaska conducted such a study to learn more about the role perspectives played in a student's performance.[6] They planted students in separate rooms to fill out positive or negative teacher evaluations and measured the performance between students in the positive-perspective and negative-perspective classes.

They found that students' perspectives have a big impact on their performance. On tests taken at the end of the section, students in the positive-perspective class

---

[6] Feldman and Prohaska. *Journal of Educational Psychology,* vol. 21, no. 4, 1979.

outperformed their classmates by 13.6%. That's the difference between a low A and a solid C.

Perspectives work. A simple perspective shift has a big influence on the results you get, but you don't need to have an always-on-super-positive-attitude. It's OK to feel bad. Emotions and feelings are part of being a human. Trying to fight emotion is like picking a fight with a rain cloud.

The bigger problem occurs when unhelpful perspectives go undetected and become a habit. In the example above, the students in the negative-class weren't consciously aware they had a negative perspective dumped on them. For them it was just a matter of fact that the teacher was poor. They spent whole class periods stuck in an unhelpful perspective, and it had a 13% drag on their grades.

To be future-proofed, you must master the skill of identifying and choosing perspectives that address reality and help you take useful action. The first step is realizing how much of a difference something as simple as a perspective shift can make.

Perspectives

Action

Results

Evidence

IT MIGHT TAKE TIME!

mechanics of perspectives

Perspectives are not about ignoring reality. They are about addressing reality and choosing the way you look at them. They are a combination of our past experiences, assumptions, expectations, and thoughts. They become the frame through which you approach problems, challenges, crises, or opportunities.

Perspectives and assumptions have a knack for becoming true. Human beings like to be right, and we especially like our deeply held assumptions to be proven true even if we're not consciously aware of what those assumptions are.

The human brain likes stability and predictability. If it receives too much feedback that its assumptions are wrong, it generates a lot of stress. Internal stress is a powerful motivator. It's the reason why subconscious, negative assumptions lead to many terrible perspectives.

Part of being future-proofed is being aware of your assumptions, tossing out unfounded negative assumptions, and consciously choosing perspectives that work with, rather than against, what you really want.

Sometimes a shift in perspectives makes a huge difference. Consider the example of a child who learns about her parents' life history, and a new level of respect emerges that fundamentally changes their relationship.

Also consider the student who makes a shift in her perspective on school and studying and sees her GPA jump a few points in a few weeks.

Other times, a shift in perspective makes a subtle difference. In the study mentioned above, students in the positive-expectation class were objectively recorded as leaning forward and keeping eye-contact more often than students in the negative-expectation class. That little change in behavior leads to a substantial, but not earth-shattering, difference in performance.

Small, sustained differences - and sometimes the earth-shattering - are the building blocks of assumption and perspective work.

If you're stuck or not getting the outcomes you want, the first place to look are your assumptions and perspectives. Fortunately, once you know the power of perspectives, you can begin to choose perspectives that work in your favor.

stop using junk

Some perspectives are junk. Here are a few:

- School is a waste of time.
- Mrs. So-and-So is a terrible teacher.
- I have too much homework.
- I don't like school.
- Everyone in school is fake.
- I'm having a bad day.
- I can't do anything right today.

These perspectives seem innocent and harmless but watch out. They are junk. They clutter the mind and make getting things done more difficult. It's like having junky sunglasses with tons of scratches on them. Toss them out.

Instead, here are a few perspectives that aren't junk:

- School gives me the opportunity to learn.
- Mrs. So-and-so is an effective teacher.
- Homework is easy.
- I like school.
- Everyone in school is doing the best they can.
- I'm having the best day of my life.
- Everything I do today is going to work out.

Changing perspectives is not about being an optimist or a pessimist. It's about being a pragmatist. Changing perspectives works. The second group of perspectives are cheesy, perhaps a stretch, and probably some you'd consider not to be true.

Whether or not you believe them is besides the point. You've got to try on the perspective, let it sink in, and then take a look around.

Try it. Take a minute and think to yourself, "This is the worst day of my life."

I'm sure you could come up with a list of ten or more reasons why this day was horrible. Here's some space to write:

Take a deep breath. Shake it off. Now think to yourself, "This is the best day of my life."

Crazy what comes to mind, isn't it? I'm sure you could probably come up with another list of all the good things that happened today. Here's some space. Go for it.

MUST
WASH
HANDS

to stay healthy, wash your hands

Perspectives can be viral. Someone casually mentions how difficult an assignment is. A student dumps on a teacher. A teacher says this is the hardest section of the year. You catch someone's look of boredom at an assembly.

Picking up negative perspectives from people is like picking up a virus. Someone sneezes and doesn't cover his mouth. Someone coughs on her hands and touches something. Icky perspectives spread, and they cause problems, sometimes minor, sometimes major.

People love to know what other people are thinking. Asking your friend's opinion or recommendation is a great way to pick up information. I like to know the stuff my friends are into and the books they are reading. But asking for an opinion is different from picking up assumptions and perspectives without thinking.

Daily we're offered a whole range of perspectives from family, friends, teachers, mentors, advertisers, and the culture. Perspectives can vary from the nefarious (nasty rumors) to the benign (the weather sure is nice today), but the function is the same.[7] They have an influence on your own experience and perception of others.

---

7 Susan Blackmore's book *The Meme Machine* (1999)

So be careful. Perspectives are viral. Next time you hear someone say, "This class is tough" or "You can't accomplish that," question it. Don't let their negative assumptions get in your way. When someone sneezes a negative perspective, remember to wash your hands. It will keep you healthy.

have a few go-to perspectives in your pocket

Find a handful of perspectives that fit you and make a difference. Keep them in your pocket for easy use. Like different pairs of sunglasses, you've got to find those that work for you.

All the little events in our lives take on meaning only when we put them in context and see them through a perspective. So the perspectives you use most often are important.

When you notice yourself stuck thinking about everything negatively, having a few go-to perspectives in your pocket makes an immediate difference.

laughing is good

Sure there are times when things need to be taken seriously. But most people take themselves way too seriously, and it creates a mess. It makes people afraid to swing for the fences, go after what they really want and even - gasp! - risk failure.

An even bigger drawback to having a serious perspective by default is that when something important does come up, more often than not, you've already spent your energy. Like someone who cries wolf too often, taking everything too seriously backfires. And besides, it's just not that fun.

Having a go-to humor perspective eliminates stress, puts a smile on your face, and gives you permission to keep going. Being able to laugh is a gift. Especially if you can laugh kindly at yourself. It frees the soul and calms the mind.

One go to perspective that I keep in my pocket is "Life is a comedy." When I get a tough phone call that could get me down, I look for the comedy in it. When I'm creating the next stage in a project, I look at "What would make this ridiculously fun to do?" When faced with a challenging call, "What's the funny part in this?" It works for me.

When the homework monster has got you down or a tough conversation is weighing on you or you're hesitating doing something that you really, really need to do, go for a ready-made humor perspective. Create one that works for you. Remember, laughing is good.

fire the ferocious internal critic

Fire your ferocious internal critic. It's just a perspective that pretends to be helpful but stands in the way. You don't have to argue or fight against the internal criticism, just ignore it.

When writing her college essay, Monica constantly did battle with her internal critic. "You're not good enough." "You can't get into a decent school." "What college would want to accept someone like you?"

It was harsh.

To move forward, she had to take the trash-talking-ferocious-little critic and fire her. It was simple.

"Trash-talking-ferocious-little critic, you're fired."

Like Donald Trump, send away the losing contestant with a trite statement on his performance or character and move on.

If the critic happens to come back, repeat the process. There's no need to get down on yourself. Just remember to be alert and fire the critic again (and again) if needed. Soon enough, it fades away and the excitement of what you're doing takes center stage.

drink a glass of water

People often aren't upset at who or what they think they are. For example, sometimes students will come to class in a bad mood with no real apparent reason. Perhaps they didn't get enough sleep. Perhaps they are bored. Perhaps they don't especially like the teacher. And perhaps they are dehydrated and just need to drink a glass of water.

Not many students carry a water bottle during school. Drinking fountains are great but not often around. Most students don't drink water at lunch. If you're having a bad afternoon, perhaps it's not the teacher or the material or whatever you think it is that's getting you down. Perhaps all you need to do is drink a glass of water.

Negative perspectives often work the same way. It's sometimes hard to figure out what exactly is causing the problem.

If you're stuck and not getting where you want to go, try drinking a glass of water. Sometimes it's all that's needed.

jet-lag

Jet-lag happens when you take a plane to a new time zone and your internal clock has to adjust to local time. Your body moved but your mind is still behind.

Perspective shifts sometimes work the same way. There's both personal (internal) jet-lag and relationship (external) jet-lag.

Personal jet-lag happens when you've made a perspective shift or breakthrough in one area of your life. The shift has to work its way through the other areas. It's like learning that you've been nominated for a big award or you got into your dream program at your dream college. You now need to come to terms with how it's going to affect the rest of your life.

Perhaps you've just found out you're going to be captain of the varsity team, you got the lead role in the play, or you scored a 35 on the ACT. Each of these things have an impact on everything else. Personal jet-lag can be even more subtle and powerful, like realizing how important following your dream is and your dedication to putting in the work. The other areas of your life have to catch up.

Relationship jet-lag happens when one person in the relationship has made a big change, but the other person still expects him to be how he used to be. This kind of jet-lag happens a lot in classrooms.

Perhaps you've taken on a positive perspective with a teacher, but she may still view you as the pouting kid in the back row. Your teacher and classmates are used to the C-worthy-effort, but now that you've been putting in A-worthy-effort, there's a gap between your performance and everyone's assumption of you.

Perhaps you've decided to not get so stressed out, but your friends are used to you being a ball of stress.

Understanding jet-lag avoids a lot of frustration. You've just got to give things a little time and the jet-lag naturally goes away. Sometimes it's helpful to address it directly, but most of the time you've just got to stick with the new you.

It's like a software update. After awhile old programs get stale and need a redesign. When the update is happening, be patient. Everything will catch up and be even better than before.

perspectives and the college application

Before you tackle the college application process, write out all the assumptions, perspectives, things you heard from others, beliefs, and expectations.

Brainstorm. Keep writing. Let the ideas flow.

Most likely you've got a pretty big list of perspectives, both useful and useless. Toss out the useless perspectives, and clarify the perspectives that are useful.

Below is an example of a helpful versus unhelpful perspective in action. It's a great idea to speak to one or two professors in the department you're interested in, but often the first reaction of students is fear.

They say to themselves, "What am I going to say? Why would a professor want to speak with me? It's going to be awkward, and do professors really have the time to speak to a high school student?"

Don't buy the negative perspective. If you wallow in it too long, you won't connect with a professor and gather more information to make the decision between schools easy.

Instead, try this perspective: "I can't believe how easy it is to find a department's phone number, pick up the phone, and speak with a professor. What a great opportunity to learn a little more about the school! Professors are people who have dedicated their lives to educating young people and of course they'd be more than willing to speak to me and be helpful."

Go ahead. Choose a perspective and make the call. Making the phone call isn't about kissing butt or trying to butter-up a professor. If you're trying to game the system, people will feel it. It's really about getting as much information about a school as you can to find out if it's a good fit. Professors genuinely care about students, and they want to make sure that you have answers to your questions.

Remember, applying to college isn't about getting into the most prestigious school, it's about finding the right fit. Taking a proactive step in finding out more information about a school and its department shows volumes about how much you care about your education and trying to find the perfect school.

patience

Passion and patience share the same root word. If you're really passionate about something, you're willing to endure a little pain and be patient to get it.

Changing a perspective is a great first step, but it's just the first step. The next step is to take action from that perspective. Here's the recipe.

Step 1: Shift perspective
Step 2: Take Action
Step 3: Be Patient
Step 4: Repeat

Remember, it all starts with your perspective. The next chapter is on passion, then action. Get ready for awesomeness.

Passion

Skill #4: The ability to identify and follow your passion.

the age of passion

You can thank modern technology. The Internet, computers, and cell phones have made us more connected and more informed than ever before. The World Wide Web is a platform for you to send and receive information about anything around the world in milliseconds. Interested in neuropsychology? You can find and follow the latest developments with ease. Want to start a blog about the best shoes to wear? Get a following of 1,000 peers and Zappos.com might sponsor you. Call Nick Swinmurn. A cold call from Nick got Tony Hsieh to join his team and take a company from $0 to $1 billion in ten years.[8] The Internet gives you the power to go from a thousand followers to more than a million within months. You do so by pursuing your passion. Nick's story of leveraging the Internet, following his passion, and helping others is becoming more common. There is no reason this story can't be yours.

Consider Gary Vaynerchuk. In *Crush It*, Gary describes his success creating a strong fan base (and reaping impressive profits) by leveraging his passions with technology. His passions are wine and people. He

---

8 *Business Week*, December 5, 2005 "A Shine on Their Shoes"

```
              1010                    0101
            01010101                1010110
          001010010101            010101100101
        010101110110101          101011010010101
      01011100101101010       010101011001101101
     010101010101010101010  1010101010101010101011
    101011100101011001010100101011001010010101
    010110011010100110101001010101101001010111
    00101010010100 PASSION 110101100110101011011
    101001010010100110101101010101011010101010
    101⊥0101010001010100101010100110010101010
     01110101001101010111001010101010111001010
      010101010101010101010101010101010101010
       101101101101010011001001011100101010
        010101010100011001101010110101101
        1010110100101010101010111010010
         10010101010100011000110101010
          101010101011101000110101010
           101010101010101010101011101
            10101010101010101010111001
            010101011100100110011011
             11001010101110010
              0101100100101
               0101010111
                0110101
                 0101
                  01
```

rants about wine. He loves people. He used technology to teach, share, and inform others and made a mint doing it.

Buckle up, follow your passion, and believe in your mission. We're living in a world where following your passion is more than just pursuing your dreams and hoping it will work out. It's a viable business plan for making a positive impact, earning money, and helping others all at the same time.

values are at the heart of your passion

Passion comes from a Latin word meaning *to suffer*. If you're passionate about something, it means you're willing to suffer for it. It's why passion is often a characteristic of leaders and passionate people are often successful. They have a reason to endure the hard work and tough times to keep moving forward.

At the heart of passions are your values. From the Latin word meaning *to make strong,* values are what make you strong and what you think are important. Values are the fuel that helps you follow your passion. Consider Nick and Gary from the last essay. Both are extremely clear about their value of respecting and caring about people. That value infuses their companies and each interaction. It's contagious. It makes their companies thrive. If they were to forget their values and just try to make a buck, their companies would literally become weak. People who know and act on their values have the strength to follow their passions.

Here's the problem: most people live their life on autopilot and haven't spent the time thinking about *what exactly is really important in their life*. Most people know that family and friends are important. But what specifically about family and friends is important to you? What about people makes them so important? What about the time you spend with your friends do you enjoy most?

The more specific you are in your values, the better you'll be at knowing what's really important to you, which helps you make decisions on how best to spend your time and energy. To get you started, below are some examples of general versus clear values.

General Value: Family
vs.
Clear Value: Meaningful conversation with family members.

General Value: Friends
vs.
Clear Value: Friends that help me grow as a person who I love being around, just as they love being around me.

General Value: Free time
vs.
Clear Value: Time for me to pursue my interests and passion.

The more specific a value is, the more useful it will be. It's common to assume that having a value of family means having meaningful conversations, spending time

PASSION

together, and loving each other. But assuming those things and not being clear on them often leads to taking those values for granted. Values taken for granted are often forgotten.

Being clear on your values and honoring them is crucial to being future-proofed. Your values give you strength and form the foundation for your fulfillment. If you're fulfilled, you're able to follow your passions and essentially 'keep the fire stoked.'

There's magic in the act of writing down your values. To get you started, write a big list of all the important things in your life and then ask yourself the question, "What specifically about this is important to me?" Here are a few prompts to get you started:

What things are absolutely crucial to your life?

Think back to a time in your life when everything was perfect. What were you doing? What was most important to you?

What phone call would you most like to receive?

What gift would you love to give your family? Your friends? Yourself?

What would be your perfect month? Week? Day?

now that you have your values, use them

Your actions are an indication of what you really believe is important. Throughout the day you make hundreds of little decisions about how to spend your time and energy. You make decisions about what to eat for lunch. Every decision is guided by your values.

Knowing your values gives you a framework to more easily make those hundreds of small day-to-day decisions as well as the larger change-your-life-path decisions. Not knowing your values is one of the reasons so many high school students find the college application process so stressful. It's hard to make decisions about the future without a structure to know what's more important.

The key is to get clear on values. Take them for a test drive. As you hone your values, you will find yourself updating your list. You're likely to have a first draft, a more concise second version, and perhaps even a third or fourth version where you really figure out what matters to you. It's a living document.

You'll soon get comfortable making decisions based on what's truly important to you, rather than reacting to what pops up in your day. When doing so becomes a habit, you'll find yourself naturally being more proactive and effective and well on your way to being future-proofed.

the i-just-want-to-be-happy syndrome

When asked "What do you really want?" many high school students simply reply, "I just want to be happy." And let's face it: we all want to be happy. We're happy when we get what we want, and good stuff *happens* to us. In fact, that's where the word happiness comes from. It's derived from the Scandinavian word *hap*, meaning *fortune, chance, or luck*. We're happy when good things *happen* to us.

Most people, however, misunderstand what scientists and researchers have proven to lead to long-term happiness. That misunderstanding is a problem because students consistently rate the desire to be happy as their number one goal and their primary form of motivation. To fully understand the implications of the problem and the solution, let's take a look at the three widely accepted strategies of happiness identified by scholars.

- Pleasure: Getting what you want, maximizing pleasure, and avoiding pain.
- Engagement: Being completely engaged in an activity that leads to a decreased sense of time and a bolstered sense of well-being (Also called Flow).
- Meaning: Taking action based on following a purpose and achieving a mission.

Guess which one over 90% of students identified as their preferred strategy of happiness, yet has been proven to backfire over the long-haul?

You guessed it. Pleasure.

The 2.5 billion dollars spent annually to convince high school and college students that getting the "coolest stuff" will make them both "cool and happy" works. Most students believe that pleasure is the best path to happiness and will go to great lengths to achieve it. Over the long run, students who identify most with pleasure as happiness suffer from feeling less fulfilled and less motivated. It's as if they continually need bigger and better things and experiences to consistently feel happy.

Rosaria Gabriele of Bucknell University recently published a study that focused on the relationship between which form of happiness students most identified with and their academic performance, involvement in extra-curricular activities and community, and clarity of career plans. The results were dramatic.[9]

Pleasure, while the most popularly endorsed form of happiness, did not have any positive correlation to any educational variables. Those students who identified engagement as a strategy of happiness were twice as likely

---

[9] Rosaria Gabriele. "Orientations to Happiness: Do They Make a Difference in a Student's Educational Life?" *American Secondary Education*. Spring, 2008: Pages 88-104.

to participate in extra-curricular activities and get involved in their community. The most striking finding, however, is those students who identified meaning as a strategy of happiness were three times as likely to perform well academically as well as have clarity about their career plans.

Wanting to "just be happy" is hollow and not a value that leads to worthwhile passion or action. The joy from working on a worthwhile project is ten times more satisfying than chasing after pleasure. Students who are future-proofed understand that hard work and pleasure is a result of creating meaning in their life and taking action to follow it.

the meaning of life

The vision stories that you created in Chapter Two are some of the most important documents you'll create. Start to include your values and you'll start to create mini-mission statements. Combining mission statements with passion is the recipe for giving your life meaning.

Creating meaning for your life is an essential component of being future-proofed. As an example of being future-proofed, few have a story as intense as Viktor Frankl, a Jewish Holocaust survivor and author of *Man's Search for Meaning*. Frankl wrote about how his survival depended on knowing what he was living for and applying it to each day, each moment.[10] He knew his values, often keeping the image of God or his beloved wife clear in his mind. He understood his passion and why he wanted to live. He had a mission to share what he learned. To Frankl, creating meaning in his life was essential to survival. He endured the harshest circumstances, and out of his suffering came a story of hope and unshakable resilience.

The challenge facing many high school students is waiting until there's intense pressure to take action or find out what's really important. With so much taken for

---

[10] Viktor Frankl. *Man's Search for Meaning*. Washington Square Press, 1984.

granted, it's easy to push aside the need to find meaning. By reminding yourself of your values, passions, and mission, you'll naturally create a life of meaning that leads to fulfillment and resilience.

Consider the example of Bill Baron, a life coach who specializes in helping people build their business. He's passionate about helping other businesses thrive and serving their needs. He puts in a lot of hard work. His classes and writings are filled with passion. When asked how he continues to work so hard for the sake of others Bill replies, "I really know *why* I'm doing the work that I do. When I'm clear on the reason I'm working, it no longer feels like I have to do the work. The thought is *I get to do this work*. It would be easy to slack off, but when I remind myself of the impact on other's lives - and to know that I've touched the lives of thousands of others - it makes a huge shift."

The shift that Bill experiences, from slacking off to getting excited to get to work, comes from getting clear on what's important, what he's passionate about, and why he's doing what he's doing. It's a simple formula that leads to resilience, excitement, and being future-proofed. With the certainty of a mathematical equation, if you take those steps, you too will realize the mind-blowing experience of living a life filled with meaning.

passion and the college application

Students who know and follow their passion are better prepared to pick schools that fit their talents and personality. They also statistically have a better chance of getting into their first choice.

If you know what's important to you, it's easier to know what schools will and won't fit. If you follow your passion, you're going to gain experience in a specific area and become a mini-expert in it. College admission officers aren't necessarily looking for well-rounded students.

Getting good grades in all your subjects and having varied interests is helpful, but colleges don't want a class full of well-rounded students. They want a well-rounded class of students each passionate about their interests. Admission officers are looking for mini-experts.

Consider the example of Max, a junior, who loved cars. He loved thinking about them, drawing them, and learning about their mechanics. He even built and raced them. Max's passion was clear, but ironically, Max didn't consider himself passionate about cars or knew how his interest applied to school.

Max also wasn't getting great grades, and he didn't see the link between getting good grades and pursuing his love of cars. What does English have to do with a combustion system?

Nothing.

Much of what you learn in school will have nothing to do with what you end up doing in life. However, school is the gateway and foundation for you to do anything else you want.

The question Max had to answer was whether he was willing to suffer a little in English, pay better attention, and get a better grade for the ultimate goal of creating awesome cars? He was. It was clear that his passion for cars could get him motivated to earn the grades he needed to earn to get into a good college.

Once Max put all of his school work within the context of following his passion(designing cars) he immediately gave new meaning to his work. An English assignment no longer was a meaningless task randomly assigned to ruin his day. It turned into another step on his path to making cars.

While Max shifted his perspective and moved into action, the results followed close behind. Within the semester his grades went from C's to B's. By senior year, he was regularly earning A's, but his SAT scores were still low.

He was, however, clear on his passion. He had extensive experience with cars, and he wrote a great application essay. The result: Max got into a great school that boasted of having students with SAT and GPA averages many points above his own.

Max got into a great school because he was an expert in one thing. He knew cars. He used his passion as a source of motivation. He improved as a student. He still wasn't the best at standardized tests and didn't have a stellar GPA, but it didn't matter. His focus and expertise also made him a strong candidate for an engineering program. By following his passion, Max made himself a strong applicant, and you can do the same.

Action

Skill #5: The ability to take consistent action.

there is no neutral

There's a myth that three speeds exist: going forwards, staying put, or going backwards. The reality is that only two speeds exist: forwards and backwards. There is no neutral.

Because time always marches on if you aren't taking action, you're going backwards. You can change your perspective as often as you want. You can tap into your passion until you're ready to burn up. You can find the root cause and assumption that's been holding you back for years. But it all doesn't matter until you put it into action.

Action may look different at different times. Sometimes you really need to take a nap. Sometimes you need to take a break. Sometimes you need to take a walk around the block or get a drink of water.

Deep down you know the action that you most need to take.

It's time to get moving.

turn action into habit

Each action reinforces habit, whether good or bad. What you did in the past is the best indicator of what you will do in the future. It's why changing behavior can sometimes be challenging. Habits are powerful. Students who earn A's are more likely to keep earning A's. Students who fail are more likely to keep failing. When you're trying to change your patterns and habits, you've got to go gentle with yourself and focus on one action at a time.

When you take it one step at a time and consciously make new habits, you naturally shift your attention to creating a system that's going to work over the long-run. Creating systems is a good place to be looking. It's your best chance of being both effective and sustainable.

The good and bad news about habits is that they tend to stick. It's bad news if your habits are horrible. It's great news if you're habits are useful and make your life easier.

Step by step, small action by small action, by taking positive actions you'll turn a bad habit into one that serves you. You'll get into a positive cycle that frees up more time and energy for you to create other positive habits.

One time events or actions rarely make a positive dent on a situation. What you're really aiming for is to create a set of simple habits that get you where you want to go. Getting into that flow of life isn't just useful and effective, it will surprise you with how fun creating new habits and systems can be.

GOALS

ARE OVER RATED

goals are overrated

Goals are overrated. How many times have you heard that writing down your goals is the first step to making them come true?

How many lists with well-intentioned goals get left in a binder, only to be found again at the end of the year?

How many times have you heard "You need to have your goals in place?"

Too many.

Forget about goals. They lead to stress and disappointment. They cause more problems than they solve. More often than not, students set a handful of goals at the beginning of the year and forget about them in a week. The unfortunate students slip back into their old patterns of stress and bad habits.

The first problem with goals is that the word "goal" implies a race, competition, or challenge. With every goal created also comes an obstacle standing in the way that needs to be overcome. Think of the major goals you've made in your life. They all involve a challenge outside your control or something that is left to chance. Caring deeply about things outside our control creates so much stress that it's often easier to forget about the goal all together. Plus, if you pin your motivation to goals, you're setting yourself up to be addicted to the ups and downs of results.

I often hear students say they don't want to apply to this college or try that activity because they are afraid they will fail, won't be accepted, and won't reach their goals. If a goal is getting in the way, toss it out.

The second problem with goals is that they place too much emphasis on the moment of achievement and usually take away time from thinking about the process and the actual work that's going to be required to get there. It's like saying you want to be a state champion without wanting to put in the hours of dedicated work that it requires. Somehow writing down a goal and believing in it is all that's necessary. It's not.

Ironically, goals are not a finish line but a starting point. Goals have one limited positive use, to gain clarity on what you want to achieve.

Once you have a compelling vision, the next step is to take a step back and ask yourself about *the actual process and habits you will need to develop to accomplish it*.

Then your job is to focus completely on the process. Use the goal as a jump-start to motivate yourself if you need it, but realize it's the force of your habits that will be the engine getting you where you most want to go.

outcomes

Instead of making goals, think about crafting outcomes. An outcome implies a system. A goal comes with great effort and may need a bit of luck. An outcome can be effortless. To get a goal, you have to beat the goalie. An outcome can be a natural consequence, but a goal requires a lot of hard work. An outcome can be duplicated with ease, while a goal is a one time hurrah.

However, not all outcomes are equally useful. In order to make an effective outcome, it has to meet these four criteria:

1. Is it stated in the positive?
2. Can you start and completely control the process of finishing it?
3. Does it have a good time to size of task ratio?
4. Can you measure the outcome?

Let's look at two common goals - "I want to get all A's" and "I want to have better friends" - as an example of how to turn goals into effective outcomes.

The I-want-to-get-all-A's goal is a master at stressing out students and making them feel like failures. Let's check it against the four criteria and see why:

1. Is it stated in the positive?

Yes. At least it's better than the "I-don't-want-to-earn-a-bad-grade goal"

2. Can you start and completely control the process of finishing it?

    No, although you can do a lot to influence your grade, the final grade comes from the teacher, not you. You can't completely control the process, and this is where having the goal of getting all A's often creates more stress than it relieves.

3. Does it have a good time to size of task ratio?

    No. It's too big to be effective. It's much better to break it down into months, weeks, or even days. This is why the goal of getting A's often gets lost in the rush of a school year.

4. Can you measure the outcome?

    Yes, at least you can measure the outcome.

To make the I-want-to-get-all-A's into an effective outcome, you must ask yourself, "What can I completely control that will most likely lead to this goal?" Then break that action down into weeks, even days. Here are some examples of effective outcomes students have created:

- I want to turn in all my assignments completed and on time this week.
- I want to talk to all my teachers about how I am learning and my progress once a month.
- I want to study for each test this month two days before the test for an hour or more.

These outcomes focus attention and energy on the action that will be immediately useful and lead to better grades. Once you know your outcome, focus on the individual actions and aim to create long-term habits.

If you made those effective outcomes into habits, the A's will come. I've seen it hundreds of times. You can trust that if you make great habits, the results will follow.

The I-want-better-friends goal is a pro at making students feel lonely and rejected. Let's see why:

1. Is it stated in the positive?

    Yes. At least it's a good start.

2. Can you start and completely control the process of finishing it?

    No, you can't control whether someone wants to be your friend.

3. Does it have a good time to size of task ratio?

> No. There are no tasks implied by the goal. It's like a wish.

4. Can you measure the outcome?

> No. You can't measure whether someone is a better friend than someone else. It's a goal whose criteria will probably never be met.

It's clear why the I-want-better-friends goal causes so much frustration. So many people are lonely yet don't do anything to reach out to others. Here are a few examples of effective outcomes from the starting point of a goal to have better friends:

- I am going to call my friends once a week to see if they want to hang out.
- I will find three ways I can be a better friend this week and follow through.
- I will reach out to two new people this week.

You can see how these outcomes imply action and focus on the process of being a better friend. The topic of friendship tends to get cheesy, but it's real. We all want better friends. We all want to be better friends. It's time to stop merely wishing and do something about it.

recipe for good grades

If you want getting better grades to be easier, you have to do three things. It's a simple recipe.

- Use your planner DAILY. If your school does not provide a planner, buy one or make one in a calendar notebook.[11]
- Use the Academic Thinking Styles to help you take notes, study, and write papers.[12]
- Talk to your teachers WEEKLY.[13]

If you do these three things, I guarantee you'll get the grades you want. It's a simple recipe. Easy to follow and as close to fail-proof as these things come.

Turning grades around with this recipe takes four to six weeks. Try it for four weeks then look at your grades.

The recipe works. If you've never considered yourself a good student, get ready to. You're being a good or bad student doesn't have much to do with who you are. It has a lot to do with the habits and the actions you take. Don't confuse a behavior (not getting good grades) with an

---

[11] See page 143 on using your planner.

[12] See page 28 on Academic Thinking Styles.

[13] See page 177 on talking to teachers.

identity (being a bad student). If you take different actions you get different results.

doing your best doesn't mean much

"To do my best" is a terrible goal. When you hear students or athletes - or anyone for that matter - say, "I did my best," did they just win or lose?

They lost.

Doing your best and putting forth effort is important, but it's not a good goal. At best, it's an excuse for making people feel better about not getting what they wanted to get.

Another problem with "doing your best" is that it doesn't mean that much. You can't measure it. It's an excuse for lazy thinking, and it doesn't make the situation all better.

Instead of thinking "At least I did my best" turn your attention to what went wrong and do something different. Because the reality is you didn't do your best. You could have done something different that would have been better.

i've-just-got-to-try-harder syndrome

Students often think that if they just try harder, they will get all A's, do better on tests, and be better students. One out of five times all that's needed is to try harder. But the other four times, the I've-just-got-to-try-harder thought usually only leads to the same results at a much higher cost. You're worn out. You're spent. You feel like you've just done your best but you haven't. You've just done what you always do until the point that you're exhausted. It's not doing your best. It's just working until you're overtired.

Hard work is required. But it doesn't look like trying harder. It looks like trying something different and making sure that you follow through.

Students who get the results they want display a similar pattern. They all do things differently from what they did before, *and they did them consistently*. They didn't do the same thing harder. They did something different, and they kept it up for a few weeks until it became a habit.

Instead of thinking about working harder, think about working differently.

the too-many-goals syndrome

I'll admit it. I've made a lot of goal lists. When I'm in the goal-setting mood, I go for it. I'll write ten even twenty goals at a sitting, print them out, and pin them on the wall.

I look at the list and feel great.

But then I run into a problem. I don't know where to start. I'll even prioritized the list and create steps and sub-steps for each goal. It doesn't matter.

Having too many goals is the same as not having any goals.

With a few dozen goals, it's impossible to focus. Getting wrapped up in the goals and tracking them take more time than actually being productive.

It's better to stick to one goal at a time. Two is OK, but if you are really serious about achieving something worthwhile, focus on one at a time.

Sometimes it helps to have a simple rule to finish one goal completely before moving on to the next.

Focusing on one outcome and achieving it makes it easier to achieve the next one and the next one after that. Soon you'll realize you've achieved an impressive list without even thinking about it.

action and the college application

The college application may be the most complex and dynamic school project you've ever undertaken. It's a big deal, and the action you take now has an impact on the next four years of your life and beyond. To add even more pressure, you're competing against your peers. It's the perfect recipe for creating a lot of stress.

Yet acing the college application can be easy. The key is to break down the big goal - getting into your first choice school - into smaller outcomes. Break it down into two-week mini-projects.

Here are a few mini-outcomes to get you started:
- Create my criteria for choosing the schools I want to apply to.
- Do some research and make the list of my top ten schools.
- Write the first draft of my college application essay. (Then in the next two weeks I want to finish the second draft of my essay).
- Identify and ask two people to write my recommendations.

By breaking down the pieces into two-week chunks, you can put all your focus on that piece of the application. Do a great job, then keep moving.

Breaking down the steps into two-week chunks keeps the process moving. Even if you start the process September of your senior year, you still will have enough time.

It's brilliant to break down a big overarching project and finish it off in small pieces. You feel like you're accomplishing something along the path, and before you know it, you've taken the task through completion.

Systems

Skill #6: Your ability to create and follow systems that deliver the outcomes you want.

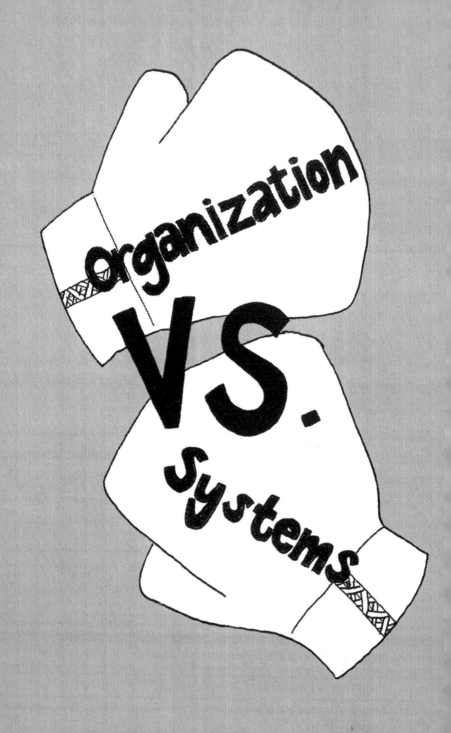

organization vs. systems

Organization is important. Organized students perform better, do more, and spend less time doing it. However, spending time "getting organized" rarely works. So often a well-intentioned student will spend an evening cleaning up a binder (or room) only to find that two weeks later the once clean binder is again messy.

Systems are the key to lasting organization. If you've tried to get more organized and failed, it's time to think in terms of systems.

Instead of thinking, "How can I clean this up?" Think "What system do I need to keep it clean?" Instead of thinking, "If only I was more organized!" Think, "What's working right now? What isn't?"

When you find yourself facing a mess or your just plain stuck, evaluate the system. Think of yourself as a mechanic or scientist. Create a system to test your idea of what would help. See how it works. Look at the results. Change the system depending on what you see. Continue to tweak and try out new ideas and structures until you get the outcomes you want.

The organization will come - and stay! - if you focus on the system. It's like the quote, "Give a person a fish and you'll feed him for a day. Teach him how to fish and you'll feed him for a lifetime." Same goes for your binder. If you clean your binder up, it will stay clean for a week.

If you create a system, it will stay clean for a year. If you continue to refine your system and get used to thinking in terms of systems, you'll create a lifetime of organization. And living a life that's organized soothes the soul and gives you a foundation to be more creative and more fulfilled.

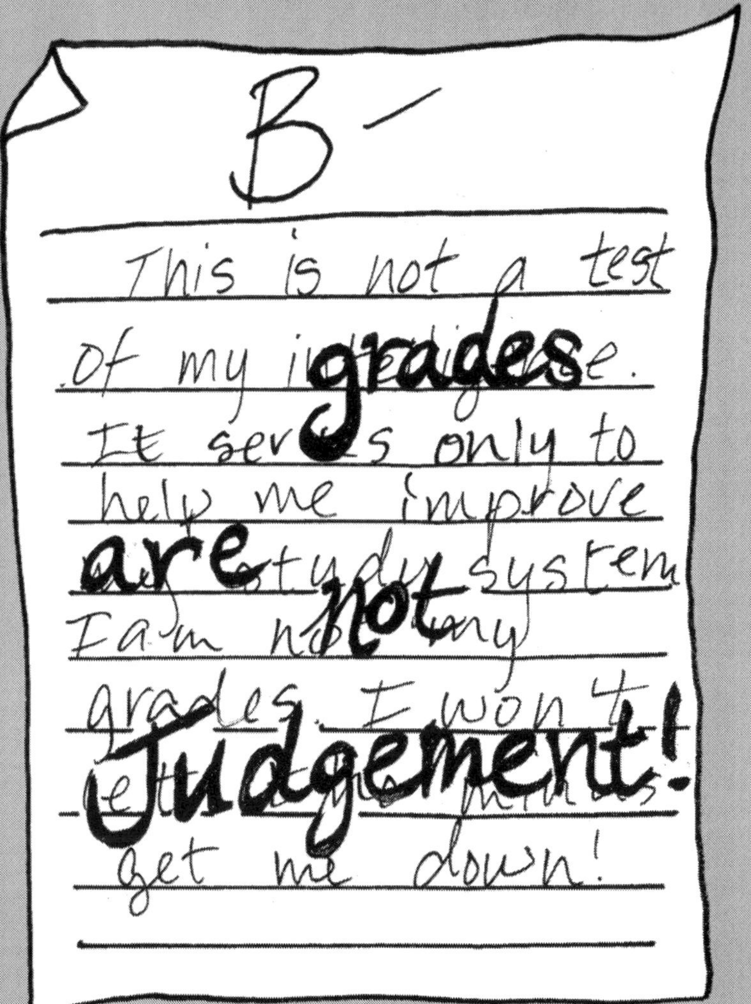

B-
This is not a test
help me improve
study system
grades. I won't
get me down!
grades
are
not
Judgement!

use grades as feedback, not judgment

Grades often tempt students to use them as little pieces of judgment on their self-worth. Good grades equal a good student. Bad grades equal a bad student.

Right?

Wrong.

Grades are not a judgment on who you are or what kind of student you are. Grades are merely feedback on the systems you're currently using to do homework, study for tests, and write papers.

As feedback, grades are really valuable. They tell you where you need to put your focus. They let you know where your system is weak. They let you know what's working. They also let you know your natural strengths.

When you realize that grades aren't personally judging you, you can use them for what they are good for: giving you information to change or keep the way you do things.

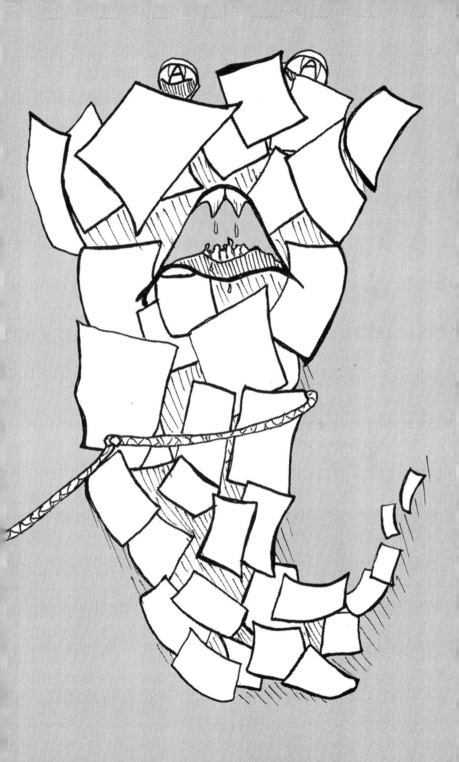

tame the homework monster

To get good grades, you have to tame the homework monster. The number of papers an average student goes through in a month is staggering. Keeping all those papers in their place can be a challenge.

To tame the homework monster, I recommend having a system with folders labeled with the action you'll need to take next.

For example, when a teacher hands you a piece of paper, there are five possible actions you need to take.

- Fill it out and complete it.
- After it's finished, turn it back in.
- Study it.
- Keep it long-term.
- Recycle (get rid of) it.

Luckily, you've created a system with structures that mimics the choices you'll need to make. You have a binder that you take with you to each class that has your planner (because you record your assignments) as well as five folders. You keep your class binders and the notebooks for each class, but this master binder saves yourself time and energy by making decisions of where to keep paper easy.

The to-do folder keeps all your to-do's in one place. It calms the mind. Gone are the days of searching for that pesky worksheet.

The to-turn-in folder is plain awesome. There's real satisfaction in filling it each night.

The to-study and to-file folders are necessary and a great stopping point between your master binder and class binders. They keep things moving.

The recycling folder is useful when you're rushing between classes. Say bye-bye to having to leaf through papers and piles and sift through stacks finding what you really need. If you know you can recycle a piece of paper, do it. Clear the clutter.

Creating a structure that mimics your actions and the decisions you'll have to make is the key to this system. Each system will have its own key, something that makes it work for you. The fun part is finding it.

vSystems

guidelines on creating systems that you'll actually use

Some quick guidelines on creating systems that you'll actually use:

1. You'll only continue using the system if it ends up saving you time and energy.

Of course, there's going to be more upfront work creating the system, thinking of your outcome, assessing the raw ingredients, and making the structures. But soon - almost immediately - you more than make up for the time you spent creating the system in the time you save.

2. Sometimes it's the details and little things that make a big difference.

If your binder (or room or study habits or time management) is a mess, take a moment to look and learn from it before you try to fix it. Often a small change, like adding a recycle folder to a binder, ends up making a big difference.

3. Looking good is a big plus.

It's true. When things look good, we're more likely to use them. A little extra time to make something look good is well worth the effort in the long run.

4. Measure your results.

What you measure, improves. If you are serious about getting organized and using systems, track how often you actually use them. Just a short check-mark each day on whether or not you used your planner improves your chances of following through. You'll also gain insights into what works and what doesn't when you measure the actions compared to the results of a system.

get done what needs to get done

There comes a certain point in time when all the life coaching, motivational talk, and inspiring words are no longer useful. It comes down to a point when you just need to get done what needs to get done.

After you do that, then you can set up a system that takes care of the problem.

But in the meantime, there comes a point when you just need to do what's in front of you.

failure = learning (when thinking in terms of systems)

Failure is not fun. It can be painful, horrible, embarrassing, or worse. But don't waste it.

When you think in terms of systems, failure becomes less personal. Sure failure can still have that personal sting, but when you take the time to learn from it, tweak your system and keep going, failure teaches you valuable lessons. In the end, it may be your failures that prove more useful and ultimately more satisfying.

I don't like to fail. I don't like to see others fail. But I do know that some of my biggest insights and some of my greatest successes came out of a direct result of failing.

use your planner

It was January, and I was giving a workshop entitled 'Stress and Grades' to 13 students during their lunch break. In the first few minutes of the workshop, I asked a series of questions.

"Who here is getting the kind of grades that you want?" Seven people raised their hands.

"Who isn't?" The other six raised theirs.

"Who is using their planner every day?" The same seven people who were getting the grades they wanted raised their hands again.

"Who isn't?" The other six students.

I wish I had it on video. There wasn't a single person who used their planner and didn't get the grades they wanted. There also wasn't a person who didn't use their planner and got the grades they wanted.

The lesson is simple. Use a planner to get the grades you want. If you don't use a planner, you won't get the grades you want.

Ask yourself the same questions. Which group are you in? Which group do you want to be in?

systems and scholarships

Students who apply to scholarships get more money for school than students who don't. It's a simple and obvious truth, yet the vast majority of students only apply to one or two scholarships.

If you create a system for applying to scholarships, you'll surprise yourself at how easy it is to apply to a dozen or more scholarships while modifying just a handful of essays.

Getting scholarships is essentially a matter of creating a system to keep track of them and applying. It's easy. Create the system, and you'll get the scholarships.

Don't and you won't apply. And if you don't apply, you can't get the scholarships.

Motivation

Skill #7: The ability to maintain motivation.

Motivation MATTERS

motivation matters

In order to get where you want to go, you will have to do hard things. You will have to face challenges that you'd rather not face. You will have to do things even if you don't feel like doing them.

However, understanding the mechanics of motivation as well as your motivation style, makes moving forward easier. Over time, if you continue to cultivate your motivation, it becomes a habit. People who have such a habit and know how to keep moving forward, no matter the circumstances, are truly future-proofed.

When you understand the nature of motivation, tasks that once seemed impossible to start cease becoming challenging. Ask any professional athlete or successful business or community leader. They have all learned how to manage their own motivation to accomplish what's important.

School presents its own set of challenges. Your homework, chores, and things you have to do are largely outside of your control. You can't really tell your teachers or parents that you don't feel like doing the homework so you're not going to do it.

The solution involves two steps. The first is to understand the mechanics of motivation and how your particular brand of motivation works for you. The second is to find your own reason for getting things done that has nothing to do with school. The next couple essays paint a picture of what you can do as a student to nurture your motivation and become future-proofed.

external versus internal motivation

Most schools and businesses rely heavily on external (or extrinsic) motivation. For schools, it's grades. If you do a good job, you get good grades. For business, it's money. If you do a good job, you get more money.

People want those things, so they do the work. It's simple. External motivation is great. You can even use it on yourself. A student I work with uses yogurt covered pretzels as little rewards after finishing tough assignments. Once you find what works for you, go for it.

However, over the past few decades numerous scientific studies have proven that external motivation only takes you so far. Internal (or intrinsic) motivation is more useful and gets people more motivated and more productive.[14] Internal motivation is a combination of three factors.

1. Choosing to undertake the task.
2. Having the opportunity to master the material.
3. Working for the sake of a larger purpose.

In other words, you work because you love to do it, regardless of an external reward for yourself.

---

14 Dan Pink. *Drive: The Surprising Truth About What Motivates Us*. Riverhead. December 29, 2009.

In the academic world, nurturing internal motivation is a serious challenge. You don't have any choice over your assignments. Due dates are dictated. Your time is micromanaged. You have to move on to the next section in the material regardless of whether you've mastered it or not. You have multiple subjects to study rather than the freedom to focus on what you love. And much of what you learn in school has little practical value in what you're going to be doing the rest of your life.

Harnessing internal motivation in any environment can be a challenge, but if you can do it in school, you've taken a huge step in being future-proofed. Previous chapters in this book, from changing perspectives and creating meaning to using outcomes instead of goals, offer a pathway for making internal motivation possible even in a traditional academic environment.

When your values and action align, and you move forward even when it's hard, you will make intrinsic motivation a habit.

There will be times when you find yourself actually enjoying your school work and having fun with projects. Catch yourself next time it happens. Remind yourself that you can actually have fun with school. Remind yourself of your larger purpose for doing well in school. The more you find yourself actually enjoying learning, the easier it is to tap internal motivation.

carrots and sticks

People are motivated to get benefits (carrots) and to avoid pain (sticks). Intrinsic benefits are an increased sense of self-worth, meaning, and enjoyment of the process. Extrinsic benefits may be better grades, being able to hang out with friends an extra hour later through an extended curfew, or getting some more cash. Intrinsic pain can be brutal, from embarrassment to feeling worthless. Extrinsic pain may be bad grades or being stuck at home, isolated from friends.

Everyone uses some combination of chasing carrots or avoiding sticks to get themselves moving. However, most people use avoiding sticks as their primary motivation style. Due dates, penalties, late fees, fear of being grounded, fear of losing your phone, fear of disappointing others, and fear of disappointing yourself are all forms of being motivated by getting away from negatives. For simple, must-get-it-done tasks, it's a useful form of motivation. It gets people moving fast and keeps people safe by getting them away from danger.

The downside is that students in this pattern usually have grades that fluctuate like zig-zags and who constantly battle to pull up their grades in one or two classes. Cycling through a state of mild (or sometimes extreme) panic, scrambling, then falling into exhaustion is not

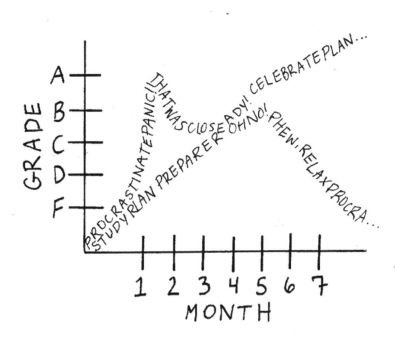

sustainable. Experiencing life as a series of fires that have to be put out is not a fun way to live. It's tiring. It's stressful. Over the long-run it's not effective. And it's not the way to be future-proofed.

Motivation towards benefits is more sustainable and the path to being future-proofed. The drawback is that it's much harder to get started, especially when the benefit may or may not happen at some distant point in the future. Working on something even when you don't have to, studying a few days before a test or a few weeks before an exam, and getting projects finished ahead of schedule are signs that you're using motivation towards benefits as your motivation style. To get into being motivated by benefits:

- Create the vision of what you want. Using your imagination to create a clear picture is essential because you are far away from your source of motivation.
- Plan and take steps to create a sustainable set of habits that will help you reach what you want.
- There will be setbacks, but the overall trend is improving, and most importantly, because you don't panic you'll be able to make decisions and create habits that you can sustain over the long-run.
- Celebrate. When you reach your goal, it's time to celebrate. Because you didn't panic, you don't feel a

need to relax. Instead, when you reach a goal from a motivation towards perspective, you feel more alive and want to do even more.

Motivation towards benefit is a forward feeding system. When you reach your goal, you're closer to your source of motivation, and you become even more motivated to continue reaching that goal. Using motivation towards and getting caught up in its cycle is an awesome experience. By creating a system that results in the outcome you want, you've future-proofed yourself. Your job now is to keep running your system, making small improvements along the way.

how to break the procrastination problem

Laziness and lack of discipline don't cause procrastination. The real cause is a lack of imagination. Sometimes it's difficult imagining if the consequences of our actions will really be that bad or that good.

- "Will it really be that bad if I put off that paper another hour?"
- "Can I really get a good grade on this?"
- "I can wait to study for math until tomorrow, I'll have more time then."

How many times have you seen people get really motivated and take action when it's too late? Just take a look at the student who furiously scans a chapter in a history book trying to cram every last bit of information into his head a few minutes before the test. It's painful to watch and even more painful to experience.

The next time you feel the urge to put off something important, think about how good it will be - actually feel the goodness - when it's actually completed.

The future will be here really, really soon. And your actions really will make a big difference. Procrastination is not a problem about being lazy, it's a problem of not having a strong imagination.

Brutal Beginning

bust through the brutal beginning

Half the work of doing a project is setting aside the time and just getting started. Especially if you want to tap into the feeling of flow, you must have the discipline (and now understanding) that it's human nature to resist the first five minutes of working.

Instead of trying to knock out the whole task in one swipe, just get through the first five minutes of writing that paper or making those phone calls. Then check in with yourself to see how it's going.

Most of the time it's only the first five minutes that are tough. In those five minutes, you give yourself time to change gears and settle into a rhythm. After you break through the beginning and get warmed up, continuing to take steps is easy.

Set a timer. After the five minutes, decide whether or not you want to continue, but make sure you bust through the beginning.

tasks and time

If you're finding it hard to get done what you need to get done and your list keeps growing, you're perhaps suffering from the wrong impression that standard to-do lists and assignment books give. Tasks don't live on their own, totally free from the time that it takes to finish them.

Try making a to-do list with the tasks scheduled on a calendar with a set amount of time allotted to each task. Although it may seem obvious, every task takes time.

Creating a list of things to do or assignments to complete is a good place to start. When you then put that list into a timeframe and judge how much time you'll need for each task, you've made a big step in creating an effective system. You've also made it much easier to get motivated to start something with enough time to finish it without a frantic dash.

You'll also have a more accurate picture of how much time something will take to finish with a set start and end time.

The bonus is that after you use a system, you get a better idea of how much time things really take, and you become better at creating realistic schedules.

Every task takes time. When you start to plan not just what you are going to do but when you are going to do it, motivation goes up and stress levels go down.

pay attention to stamina

I've seen it often. Something interesting happens to students who begin to apply the concepts of motivation and action in their lives. They get tired. They are satisfied and have accomplished more than they are used to, but they are tired. It's a different feeling from being exhausted and stressed out. It's similar to the feeling after a good workout.

It's a good sign.

Just like athletes need to develop their stamina for competition, students need to develop their study, writing, and test-taking stamina.

Studying and doing homework is not a onetime event. They take real mental resources to accomplish. Feeling tired is a good sign and means you're pressing your boundaries and building your mental resources. The more you do it, the more you practice and build up your stamina, the better you get.

Remember, when you hit your wall, push a little more. It's a good sign that you're building your stamina.

motivation and the college application

Positive, intrinsic motivation is where it's at. Colleges are looking for students who have a desire to do well not because of grades but because they love to learn and they are learning for a larger purpose.

Once you find the work that you love to do and the subject that ignites your curiosity, follow it. If you're having fun, if you're willing to put in the time to get good at it, and if it serves a larger purpose, follow it with all you've got.

You have 100% permission to follow your passion outside of school. Colleges are looking for students who demonstrate and take concrete steps in following their passion. If you are intrinsically motivated, if you go after what you love, if you're willing to put in the work, then being accepted to your dream school is secondary and just another step along a bright path.

And when you hit a bump in the road, if you have other motivation styles in your back-pocket ready to use, you'll find the college application process a breeze.

Help!

Skill #8: The ability to ask for help and gather your resources.

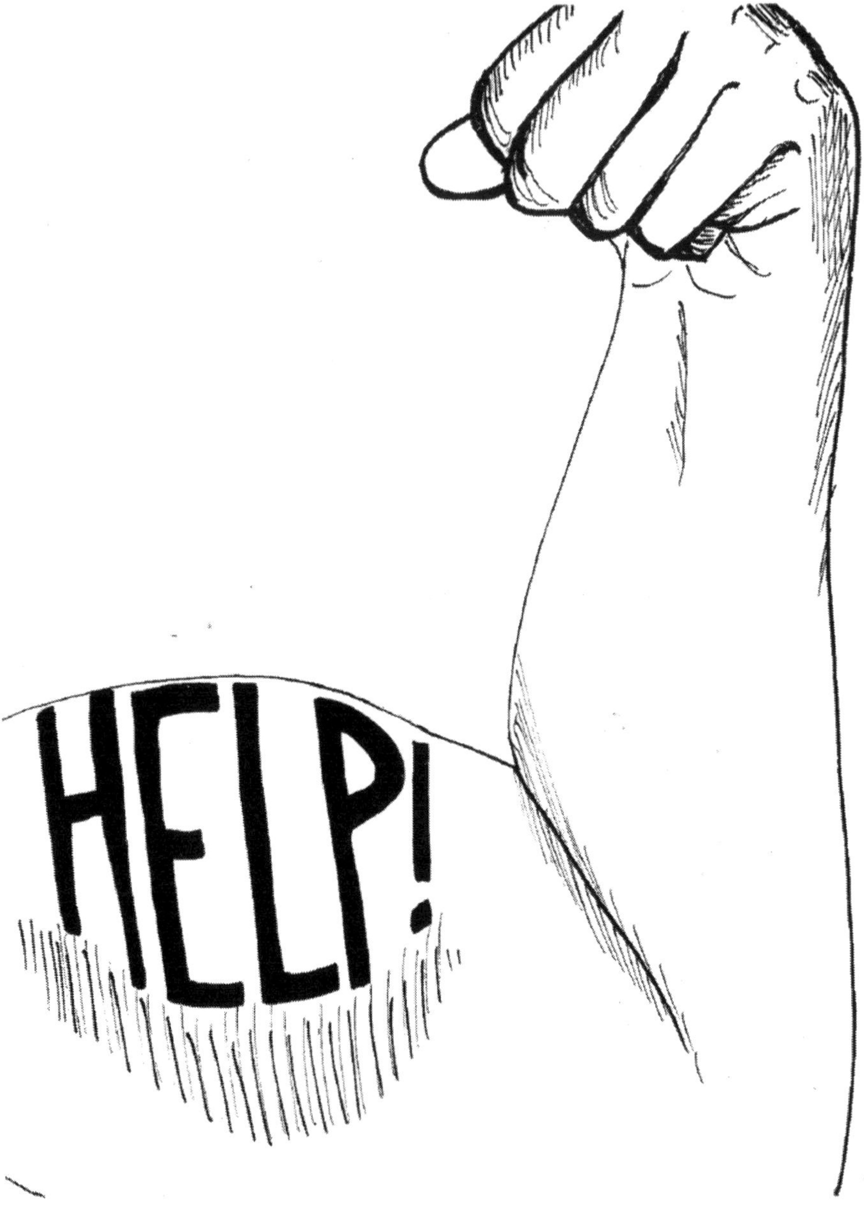
HELP!

myth: asking for help means you're weak

Don't buy into the myth that asking for help means you're weak. It's easy to fall into this trap. In high school 99 out of a 100 assignments are meant to be completed individually. Asking for help from a classmate is OK, but it soon borders on directly getting the answers, which is not OK.

Asking for help also means that you can't figure it out for yourself, and figuring out things for yourself is a big value in traditional education.

Once you graduate, however, the rules change. People who learn to ask for help and gather all their resources are more effective and successful. With technology changing, the way people work together with increased specialization and expertise, it makes sense to rely on others for knowledge and information.

The point is not to do everything yourself. The point is to know when to do it yourself and when to ask for help.

Start asking for help now. Don't wait until you graduate to start. There's so much to learn and experience in this world, and the sooner you ask for help and gather your resources, the better.

give and gather information

Don't let fear of not getting what you want stand in your way of asking for help.

You can't control whether or not someone helps you. So don't focus on it. Instead focus on what you can control: giving someone information that you need help in this area.

It's useful to give concise information on what you need and why you need it. By being clear, you make it as easy on the person to understand you. That's your job.

Your other job while asking for help is to be thoughtful, respectful, and ask what would be helpful to them.

It's not about keeping a "help score" or making sure that you immediately repay any help you get.

Your job is to give and gather information about what help you need and what help others need. From there, the natural process of being in a community and helping each other unfolds. Allow yourself to fully participate. People want to help, just as you naturally want to help others.

forget the lone-ranger mindset

Once upon a prairie there was a cowboy. He didn't need nothin' from nobody. He had everything he needed. He had his horse, a gun, and a job. He could steer hundreds of cattle across acres of green goodness, and he was a real man, right?

Wrong.

The lone-ranger doesn't exist, and it's useless to try to be one. Everyone is connected to everyone else, and the lone-ranger mindset doesn't come from the strength of doing things alone. It comes from the weakness of not trusting others.

Being future-proofed requires that you're able to work well with others. You have to learn to trust others. You have to share. You have to know what you're good at and what you're not. You don't know what you don't know, and learning to work with others helps you cover your blind spots.

Another valuable benefit of working with others and knowing what you're good at and what you're not is that you can focus on your strengths. By doing so, you not only use your talents in the best way you can, you'll be more effective and add real value to others.

money and finances

Money and finances are big topics that don't get a lot of attention in high schools' curricula. While you are in high school, making money seems like a far off reality. It's as if at some point in the distant future, you will have to make money and the best thing you can do right now is focus on your grades.

Unfortunately, that's not the case. Focusing on getting good grades is good, and it will keep a lot of options open, but the lack of financial literacy is a serious gap in current high school curricula.

If you wait until the time you graduate to learn about finances, it's too late. You've already made several important choices that have put you on a certain career path. Your first ten years out of school are so important to your long-term financial stability that hitting the ground running with an awareness of money and finances is crucial.

The bottom-line is that you need to ask for help and gather all the information you can about how to manage money and the impact of choosing certain careers on your lifestyle.

When you ask others, here are just a few suggested questions to get you started:

- Mom and Dad, I'd really like to know more about managing money. Could you show me how you do it?
- What is the financial impact of certain careers on lifestyle?
- What are the various ways of starting a business?
- What exactly is corporate culture?
- What are the next steps after I graduate from college or graduate school?
- How much does rent/mortgage cost and what's a reasonable monthly budget?
- What path do I need to take to do what you do?

Ask your parents. Ask your relatives. Ask professionals in fields you're interested in. Ask your mentor. Ask people you trust and put the pieces together.

asking for help on the College Application

Two of the most important decisions that face students are what college and career to choose. The number of options dazzles the mind. More than 8,000 colleges and universities exist in the United States. Combine that with the number of majors offered and the multitude of careers, jobs, and business options, and it's hard to know which way to turn.

Asking for help, especially from those you trust and who have more life experience, is one of the best uses of your time and their knowledge. People want to help you. People like to help out high school students. The knowledge and training that the younger generations receive is a big part of the legacy of older generations.

Believe it or not, your parents know a lot about adult life. Listening to your parents is good, really good. Your parents have a wealth of information about what life is like after school, and they are an important resource.

And don't just stop with your parents. Seek answers from your college counselor. Use the Internet to learn about different colleges, majors, and careers. Ask people in the field you want to go into. Look for the leading experts in the field. Send them an email. The best advice about how to get where you want to go is to ask people who are already there.

Relationships

Skill #9: The ability to form and maintain healthy relationships with peers and adults.

people are more important than things

The quality of the relationships you build has a direct relation to your degree of being future-proofed. Your spiritual relationship, your relationships with those closest to you, your relationships with other leaders, and people of influence have an impact on your fulfillment and effectiveness.

Everyone knows people are more important than things. Yet in the rush of school, with a constant barrage of tests and grades, that simple truth gets lost in the grade report.

It's not really the school's fault. Schools are designed to teach knowledge that can be measured. You can measure how many answers you got right on a math test. You can give a reasonable objective measurement of the analysis of an essay. But you can't easily measure your ability to build strong relationships or how well people are caring for those around them.

Just because you don't get a grade in it, doesn't mean it's not important. What skill do you think was more useful to most professionals in the past week: the ability to form and maintain healthy relationships both personally and professionally or their knowledge of geometry and calculus?

Nearly everyone will tell you that relationships were way more useful. You can substitute any other academic subject, and still your ability to maintain working, healthy relationships is more important.

Of course math is worthwhile. Students need to study it, but let's at least be real about it. Much of what you learn in high school doesn't have a direct use in your adult life. It doesn't mean that you can blow off school. Doing well in school is important. However in the rush of homework, tests, and grades, avoid the trap of thinking that your academics are more important than your relationships.

Building relationships is, and will be, extremely important. Don't lose sight of the importance of people while you're being relentlessly tested on academic subjects.

People are always more important than things.

we are all on the same team

all on the same team

We're all on the same team trying to figure things out and get where we want to go.

Your parents are on your team.

Your teachers are on your team.

The administrators of your school are on your team.

Everyone.

Everyone wants to help you.

We're all on the same team.

Let's see how this concept makes a difference in your life.

Imagine you're getting a bad grade in science. It's obvious that you aren't doing well on tests and you have some missing homework assignments.

If you assume your teacher is not on your side and is out to get you, chances are you'll not take the time to talk with her outside of class. But if you do, you'll most likely ask:

- "What can I do to get a better grade?"
- "Can I do anything for extra-credit"
- "Am I missing any assignments?"

It's pretty obvious that you care more about your grade than learning the material. Bad idea.

A much more useful approach is to assume that teachers are really on your team. They want to help you. It's a quick little perspective shift that makes a big difference. Students who approach teachers with this perspective ask different kinds of questions and get a much better response.

- "What skills do I need to learn to do better?"
- "How can I study for this next test better?"
- "What would you suggest I do to improve my performance?"

You'll get useful answers, and you'll build the student-teacher relationship. Your teachers are trying to teach you useful information. They *want* to help you.

The reality is that everyone, you and your teachers and parents and everyone else, are all on the same team. If you play like it's so, others will too.

levels of listening

Listening is an underrated skill, and there's more to listening than just paying attention. In fact, paying attention is only the beginning.

One of the core skills of life coaching, as well as being an effective leader, is to be able to listen from multiple points-of-view.

Most people listen from their own point-of-view and when they listen they think "How does what this person is saying relate to me?"

Listening like this is what most people think of as listening. It's useful, especially in a classroom when you have to take in information.

But there's another kind of listening. Instead of listening from your point-of-view, listen from their point-of-view. Instead of thinking "How does this apply to me?" think "How does what they are saying apply to them?" It's a subtle but profound shift. When you learn to listen from another's point-of-view, a whole new world opens up.

Being future-proofed requires your ability to listen - really listen - from the other person's point-of-view. When you practice this kind of listening, you'll communicate more effectively. Empathy, compassion, and curiosity arise naturally. You're able to understand a lot more about the other person. You don't take things

personally. You get yourself out of your own way, and you're more available to help.

Try it. Next time you're in a conversation with a friend, notice how often you say silently to yourself, "I want to do that too!" "That reminds me of..." "When is it my turn to talk?" Those thoughts are symptoms of listening for the sake of yourself. Recover and turn your attention to "What about this is important to them?" "I wonder what this experience must be like for them?"

You'll notice that your listening changes from trying to think of the next thing to say or trying to fix the problem to becoming curious and listening deeply. There's a big difference between these two kinds of listening.

Both levels of listening are useful. They serve different purposes. When you're in class and you need to understand the material and assignment, listening for the sake of "self" is useful. When your friend is having a hard time and you want to be there for him, listening from his point-of-view is the way to go.

speaking for their sake

Understanding the different kinds of listening is crucial to effective communication. The other half of communicating effectively is being able to speak in a way your listener understands.

The best communicators take responsibility for what they intend to say and for what their listener actually understands.

The meaning of your communication is how it's understood. Your intention is great, but it doesn't mean much. Your listener's understanding is the final judge.

Just like the different kinds of listening, there are different kinds of speaking. Talking for the sake of yourself has a certain impact. Speaking for the sake of someone else has a different impact. People can hear, even feel, the difference in the quality of your communication.

Of course, sometimes you have to talk for your sake. You have to get something you need. For most people, this kind of speaking is not a problem.

What's rarer, and much more powerful, is the kind of speaking for the sake of someone else. It doesn't have to be sappy, or sound soft and overly caring. But there's a definite shift in awareness.

It starts with being aware of the other person and his situation. The next step is to keep your intention in mind and make it easy to understand what you mean.

Sometimes it means taking more time and slowing down or picking a different time to communicate.

Ultimately, what your listener understands is your responsibility. The key to effective communication, one of the keys to being future-proofed, is your ability to both listen and speak from someone else's point-of-view.

status matters

So much of what goes on in relationships and in schools is the result of people jockeying for social status. Social status is important. We have a fundamental need to know how we fit into a community, and knowing our place and status has been part of our culture for thousands of years. The truth is we are social beings, and status is a way of organizing ourselves so we can all get along.

Low status is not necessarily bad. High status is not necessarily good. But it is bad to be stuck in either one and not be comfortable with the full range. Being humble (having a low status) is valuable. Allowing your talents to shine and speaking up for yourself (having high status) is also useful.

Middle and high school students are especially aware of status. It's the time in life when we figure out who we are and how we fit in.

Social status is so important to our identities that we're often willing to go to great lengths to protect our status.

There are two ways of boosting your status. If we consider ourselves in competition and on different teams, we boost our status by putting down the status of others. Look at all the smack talk in professional sports. If your team sucks, then my team must rock.

If we consider ourselves on the same team and in the same boat, we boost our status by raising the status of others. Look at close friends or the leaders who inspire others. They think, "I rock, and we're all in this together, so that means you must rock too."

Bullies pick on others because they think they are different. They think, "If I put you down, I raise myself up."

With the emergence of social media and the modern economy shifting to the online world, it's easier to call out bullies. It's also easier to find those who really do want to help. The old paradigm of bullying, hyper-competition, and win-lose mindset stinks. The helper, hyper-cooperation, and win-win mindset is the new way of doing business.

We each choose one of these mindsets hundreds of times throughout the day. Which choice are you making?

relationships and the college application

While you're in the middle of your college application, make things easy for your parents. The college application can create a lot of stress, especially as deadlines approach and forms need to be filled out.

Remember to listen occasionally from your parents' point-of-view. It helps to give them information in a way that they can understand even before they think they need it.

You will be heading off to college soon enough, and the time you have with your parents is precious. By focusing on building your relationship with your parents, and not getting caught up in the stress of the application, you will find navigating all the forms much easier.

In terms of your college application, your college visits are crucial. When you see the school in-person, you'll learn a lot about the college that's difficult to gather from a website or simply reading about it. You will also have an opportunity to meet students and professors. Take it! The more people you can meet and speak with, the more information you'll get about the school and the better you'll be able to make a decision about whether it's a good fit for you.

While on a college campus visit the department you're interested in. You don't have to be absolutely certain about your major to take this step. Just pick your strongest fit and go with it. Ask to sit in on a class. Perhaps there is a professor or advisor whom you can speak with. By focusing on the people, and not just the institution, you will get a better idea of what it will really be like to go there, which is valuable information to have. These are the people who you will be working with over the next four years.

Community

Skill #10: The ability to build as well as add value to your community.

build your community

Being able to build a community of people you like and trust - and who like and trust you - is essential to being future-proofed. Human beings are social beings. We thrive when we are in a community of people who love and support us. As well as helping complete high school successfully, having the support of others is one of the few major factors in determining whether or not students graduate college. Being part of a strong community helps people find jobs, launch businesses, and find stability.

Community comes from nurturing relationships and understanding what networking is and how to do it well. Networking is a skill. It boils down to three concepts:

1. Truly caring about others and seeking to help them.
2. Exchanging information and letting others know what help you need.
3. Building relationships and connecting people to other people.

The quality of the network you create corresponds to how effective and successful you become. Consider the Internet for example. Computers not connected to the web are nearly useless. Computer plugged into the web, however, have access to vast amounts of information.

In the same way, people who are not connected to others and don't take care of their relationships are simply not as effective. The network of relationships and the community you build will help you overcome challenges and open up opportunities.

Your community is one of your most valuable resources for being future-proofed.

don't keep count

Effective networking is not about keeping count of whom you helped and who helped you so that you have to keep an even score. There will be times when you help others more than they help you in return. At other times, others will help you more than you could ever help them in return.

Keeping count is not the point. Instead, it's best to focus on how you can help others and be mindful and grateful when others help you.

The more you ask yourself the question, "How can I best help you?" or "What would be helpful to you?" the better you get at connecting and helping others.

Help enough people, and you'll get all the help you need, when you need it.

one thank you a day

Gratitude is the currency of networking.

The one habit I've seen make the biggest difference in networking is the habit of writing one thank you note a day. You'll be surprised at who responds and the relationship that you can spark by simply reaching out and sending someone a sincere thank you.

Written notes of thanks are rare.

People naturally love to help high school students. Especially people thinking about their legacy and what they want to contribute to the world.

If a teacher has had a positive impact on you, thank him. If a book has made a huge difference in your life, let the author know. If a musician cuts an album that has a lot of meaning for you, write her a quick letter.

Reaching out and thanking people is a profound habit to get into. It's an invitation to spark a relationship and you'll be surprised who responds and how quickly the opportunities arise.

I've received replies from best-selling authors. I've heard back from world-renown professors, and it's lead to some great friendships that have extended throughout the years.

People deeply appreciate being thanked, especially if their work has had a tangible, positive impact on you. Getting in the habit of thanking people is a great structure to make sure you're actively building networks and planting seeds for future relationships.

start the conversation, you'll find your angels

Predicting who will help and how they will help doesn't work. Some people will go out of their way to help you. Others won't. You can't determine who will help you and who won't. So don't try.

Instead focus on simply reaching out to people. Soon you'll find your angels. You'll find people who believe in you and want to help you. They will become your advisors and allies. They will go out of their way to make sure you are successful.

Finding a mentor is one of the ways you can rapidly advance your own understanding of the world. Mentors can be teachers. They can be relatives. They can be people in your community whom you admire.

Mentors simply have more life experience and can help you see things that you may have missed. With their knowledge they can help you achieve your goals in a fraction of the time, saving you years of angst.

But to find a mentor, you have to ask. And the first step is picking up the phone and calling. It's a big first step, and one that few students do. But that's why asking for a mentor is so effective. So few actually ask, and it's an honor to help the future generation.

Pick up the phone and you'll find your angels.

Leadership

Skill #11: The ability to exercise leadership in your life and community.

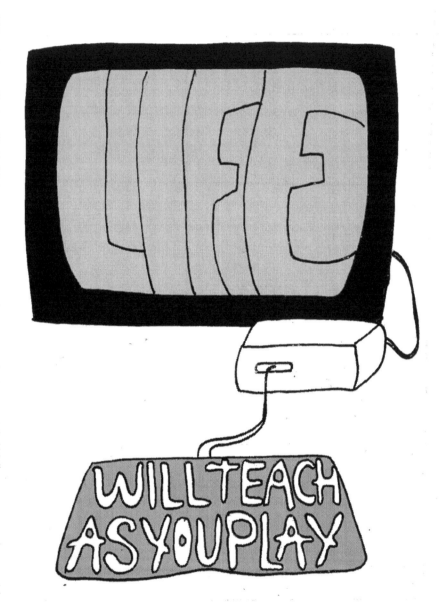

future-proofed with super powers

If you apply the principles of the previous ten chapters you will naturally step up into a leadership role in your life, in your community, and in the world. Taking an active role in creating your future is the best way to proof yourself against the challenges you will face. Once you start to fully apply yourself and engage with life, life will show the skills you need to develop what you need to know.

In the first chapter you turned your attention to the most important subject you will ever study: yourself. Knowing yourself is not just some cheesy saying that educators talk about or people write for senior messages on high school graduation cards. Taking the time to ask yourself who you are and what's your impact on other people is an act of courage. It takes guts to ask yourself about your limitations and weaknesses. It's sometimes frightening to speak out with confidence and take steps to live the life you've dreamed of.

In the second chapter you learned about the importance of creating a vision. The quality and clarity of the vision you create for yourself has a direct impact on the quality of the results you get. Once you create a vision more compelling than any present circumstances, and you continue to take steps towards that vision, soon your vision will match reality. When it does you'll have the sensation of living a dream that you've dreamed. I know. I've done it. It's a surreal experience that's both humbling and exciting with the possibilities of creating something even more magnificent.

In Chapters Three through Ten you learned concepts and skills to apply in your own life to become future-proof. If you apply these skills in your life, you will naturally do better on the college application. Your stress levels will naturally lower. Your GPA will increase. You will get along better with your parents. You will have more confidence in yourself. You will be a better friend to others, and you will find you have better friendships. You will make a positive difference in your life now, and you'll also be building a foundation that will have an exponentially positive impact on your future. The quality of who you are becoming is a direct result of what you choose to do with your life. You just need to keep taking the next step. You can trust yourself, and you can trust the world to teach you what you need to know.

The biggest challenge is believing that life can be as good as you imagine it to be. The challenge is real. Sometimes it's difficult to continue to move forward, to take those risks, and to really believe in yourself. Yet that's exactly what's required.

We live in an age when technology makes what seemed impossible not just possible but easy. You can have a videoconference with people scattered throughout the world with just a computer and a good Internet connection. You can make a film, upload it to the web, and have millions of people watch it at their leisure. Technology gives you super powers. Being future-proofed requires both an understanding of yourself, the creativity to use technology to fit your purpose, and the guts to keep taking action.

Being future-proofed is much more than just meeting challenges and exploring opportunities. It's about finding your calling and being who you know you were meant to be. It goes beyond finding a job or doing well in your career. It's about recognizing your calling and following it with all you've got. The world needs you to be your best self. The world needs you to be future-proof.

Deep down you know what you really need to do. Now is the time to do it.